PRAISE FOR
PERMISSION TO LIVE FREE

"In a world that celebrates sameness, Jackie Greene's ministry and mission untether us from fear and gives us permission to be the unique individuals that God intended. Each chapter of this book will shake you awake from the doldrums of comparison and complacency then challenge you to live out your God-given design freely and fully. Instead of melding seamlessly into the mold, you'll discover the power of accepting your unique identity and then surrendering it fully to Jesus Christ. More than ever before, we need these words. And we need this work. Write on, Jackie. Write on."

—PRISCILLA SHIRER, BIBLE TEACHER AND AUTHOR

"There are few things more empowering than when someone who has experienced liberation turns around and gathers those who are still bound. Dr. Jackie Greene is a force unleashed who has generously laid her heart open for us all to experience freedom. She shows that God's perfect plan for our lives unlocks unimaginable joy, creativity, grace, and strength."

—SARAH JAKES ROBERTS, PASTOR AND
AUTHOR OF *WOMAN EVOLVE*

"*Permission to Live Free* is an amazing book written by my friend Dr. Jackie Greene. Through these pages, Jackie will help you discover freedom to achieve your God-given destiny, fill your life with meaning, and become the masterpiece He created you to be."

—VICTORIA OSTEEN, CO-PASTOR OF LAKEWOOD CHURCH

"*Permission to Live Free* needs to be in everyone's library as a go-to book. It reminds us that God created us priceless masterpieces. BE YOU ON PURPOSE!"

—REAL TALK KIM, PASTOR, ENTREPRENEUR, AND MENTOR

"In her book my sister, Dr. Jackie Greene, gives us permission to remove the labels and stories that we've told about ourselves and find freedom to walk in the version of ourselves that God originally designed. I recommend it without reservation for girls and women everywhere."

—TASHA COBBS LEONARD, RECORDING ARTIST AND PASTOR

"In *Permission to Live Free*, Dr. Jackie Greene takes readers on a journey from bondage to freedom. Sharing vulnerably from her own story, she invites readers to find freedom from the ways they are bound, tangled, and stuck. Lighting the path before them, she ushers readers into the life-giving way of living with permission."

—BOBBY SCHULLER, LEAD PASTOR OF *HOUR OF PRAYER*

"*Permission to Live Free* was written for women everywhere who long to know what the voice of God is saying over them and step boldly into their calling. From the boardroom to the carpool line, this book will equip and empower you to lead with confidence in whatever space you walk into, firmly anchored in the truth of who God called you to be."

—HAVILAH CUNNINGTON, FOUNDER OF TRUTH TO TABLE

"The reassuring truth about Dr. Jackie Greene is that what she is giving to the world, she is to her home and family and friends first. Her message has done a work in me, and I know it will continue to change lives around the world."

—CHANDLER MOORE, RECORDING ARTIST

"My friend Jackie has written a book that I know is going to challenge you, stretch you, and bless you. Through her words you will find the areas of your life where *you* have blocked yourself from moving on. This book will help you get out of your own way and finally give yourself permission to live free!"

—TIM ROSS, HOST OF *THE BASEMENT* PODCAST

"Dr. Jackie Greene has taken the word 'permission' and revolutionized its meaning for the twenty-first-century woman. We believe this is the first of many books she will pen giving the reader permission to encounter and collide with the destiny assigned to them at birth."

—MATTHEW AND MONA THOMPSON, PASTORS
OF JUBILEE CHRISTIAN CHURCH

"In *Permission to Live Free*, Dr. Jackie Greene gives readers permission to become the very best versions of themselves—to become who God designed them to be. And I'm excited to see how the world is going to be impacted by those who read this book!"

—DHARIUS DANIELS, PASTOR OF CHANGE CHURCH

"This book is an invitation for us all to go on a journey: to truly live free, to give ourselves the permission we desperately need and want, to rest from striving, and to be free not only from the noise of the world but from the noise of the lies we've come to believe about ourselves."

—IRENE ROLLINS, AUTHOR OF *REFRAME YOUR
SHAME*, PASTOR, AND RECOVERY ACTIVIST

"A powerful, timely message that will change the trajectory of your life. Dr. Jackie is honest, vulnerable, wise, insightful, and reminds us that being who we were created to be is the best gift we can give ourselves and our world."

—JIMMY ROLLINS, AUTHOR OF *LOVE OUTSIDE
THE LINES*, PASTOR, AND SPEAKER

"Having had the privilege of knowing Dr. Jackie Greene personally, I can attest to the fact that she lives so freely in the life God has created for her. I can't think of a better person to write this book. *Permission to Live Free* is a beautiful guide to walking through the day-to-day of our lives and will be a gift to anyone who reads it!"

—CHRIS DURSO, AUTHOR OF *THE HEIST*

"Dr. Jackie Greene bravely and vulnerably shares powerful insights that will serve to ground you in your God-centered identity. More than just instruction, this book is an invitation to a whole new way of thinking and living, a hope-filled reminder that you don't have to settle for anything less than what God desires for your life."

—DAVID DIGA HERNANDEZ, EVANGELIST

"In *Permission to Live Free*, Dr. Jackie Greene reminds us that we are not a mistake by helping us reclaim the beauty in every area where shame has distorted God's truth. This book is needed by all of us."

—NONA JONES, PREACHER, BUSINESS EXECUTIVE,
AND AUTHOR OF *KILLING COMPARISON*

"With the turn of each page, it was as if Jackie was taking me by the hand and urgently leading me to a place where she had already been, refusing to leave me behind. Both captivating and liberating, *Permission to Live Free* is the book that the little girl within is begging you to read."

—KATY KAZADI, WRITER, ARTIST, AND TEACHER

"Each page offers you the courage to rise above every restriction established by society, familial dynamics, and even personal limitations. As Dr. Jackie vulnerably bears her truth, you'll find hope from her story and freedom within yours."

—LABRYANT AND PHINEKA FRIEND,
PASTORS OF BELONG CHURCH ATL

"Dr. Jackie Greene inspires us in these pages to live in total freedom. This book brilliantly dares readers to believe the truth of who they are in Christ, . . . permitting us to walk in our unique identities with authority and *freedom*."

—TIM AND BRELYN BOWMAN, PASTORS

"I love this book because it will give the necessary tools and courage to those who are afraid to really live in freedom!"

—MICHELLE WILLIAMS, AUTHOR AND SPEAKER

PERMISSION
TO
LIVE FREE

Living the Life God
Created You For

DR. JACKIE GREENE

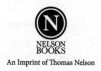

NELSON
BOOKS
An Imprint of Thomas Nelson

Permission to Live Free

© 2023 Dr. Jackie Greene

Published in Nashville, Tennessee, by Nelson Books, an imprint of Thomas Nelson. Nelson Books and Thomas Nelson are registered trademarks of HarperCollins Christian Publishing, Inc.

The author is represented by Alive Literary Agency, www.aliveliterary.com.

Thomas Nelson titles may be purchased in bulk for educational, business, fundraising, or sales promotional use. For information, please email SpecialMarkets@ThomasNelson.com.

Unless otherwise noted, Scripture quotations are taken from The Holy Bible, New International Version®, NIV®. Copyright © 1973, 1978, 1984, 2011 by Biblica, Inc.® Used by permission of Zondervan. All rights reserved worldwide. www.Zondervan.com. The "NIV" and "New International Version" are trademarks registered in the United States Patent and Trademark Office by Biblica, Inc.®

Scripture quotations marked NASB are taken from the New American Standard Bible® (NASB). Copyright © 1960, 1962, 1963, 1968, 1971, 1972, 1973, 1975, 1977, 1995, 2020 by The Lockman Foundation. Used by permission. www.Lockman.org

Scripture quotations marked NKJV are taken from the New King James Version®. Copyright © 1982 by Thomas Nelson. Used by permission. All rights reserved.

Scripture quotations marked NLT are taken from the Holy Bible, New Living Translation. Copyright © 1996, 2004, 2015 by Tyndale House Foundation. Used by permission of Tyndale House Ministries, Carol Stream, Illinois 60188. All rights reserved.

ISBN 9781400241903 (eBook)
ISBN 9781400241859 (HC)

Library of Congress Control Number: 2022051712

Printed in the United States of America

23 24 25 26 27 LBC 5 4 3 2 1

I dedicate this book first to my Heavenly Father, who I affectionately call Daddy. Thank You for healing my brokenness and consistently exposing me to a love that changed everything about me.

To my husband and best friend, without you the story of permission would still be untold. The life of freedom that is now my home would simply be a place I wished to reside but felt too afraid to go after. You fought for my freedom and I will never forget.

To my sons, my little hearts, with every breath I choose to walk worthy of the call so that you will never have an excuse not to do the same.

Finally, I dedicate this book to every woman who has already made a decision to wave the banner of freedom high, and to every woman who will pick up this book and make the choice to do the same. I celebrate your courage to go after the life of freedom God created you for. It's the only way to truly live, and I want you to know you have full permission!

A woman lives with permission when she makes the choice to be precisely and fully who she was created by God to be.

Choosing to live with permission, day after day, is the best choice you will ever make.

CONTENTS

FOREWORD
by Travis Greene

DIFFERENT TYPES OF DRIVERS EXIST IN THE WORLD. SOME
hold their steering wheel with two hands. When approaching
a yellow light, their instinct is to slow down, anticipating that
red is coming. They take any necessary precaution to avoid
an accident. This care could be due to a previous wreck or
knowledge gained in driver's ed. Something in their past has
persuaded them that it's safest to be hesitant as a driver. I com-
mend these drivers for keeping our roads safer.

Others, like myself, are a little riskier. We see yellow lights
as an opportunity to speed up. The red light is our enemy, and
yellow indicates that it is soon approaching. We believe that
red's sole purpose is not to keep us safe but rather to slow us
down. This is our philosophy, our silly opinion, our immature
persuasion.

While drivers react differently to the yellow light, there
has never been any doubt of the purpose of the green light.
Green means go! And while I have grace for anyone's interpre-
tation of the yellow light, remaining still in the face of green is

beyond my understanding. There is traffic waiting for you to move forward. What is causing the delay? Is there something pulling your attention away? Are you nervous about what's ahead?

If you have breath in your lungs, your life has a purpose. There is an expectation for you to drive. God will be your compass; He's more reliable than any manmade navigation system. But He will not press the gas pedal for you because He has equipped and empowered you to drive. Behind you is a traffic jam. Each vehicle represents someone you are called to lead—your children, your church, your coworkers, your neighbors. Until you look up and move forward, they will remain at a standstill.

The Bible is for us what a warranty is for our car. Vehicles also have manuals—and for us, our manual is Permission to Live Free. God has anointed my wife and co-pastor, Jackie, to move forward—after years of stall outs and hesitation in the face of green lights. Through her personal journey she's obtained insight into how to press on and live freely as God intended, and she graciously shares that wisdom with you in this book. Get ready to accelerate faster than ever. The light is green. You have permission. It's time to go!

TRAVIS GREENE, LEAD PASTOR OF FORWARD
CITY CHURCH AND GOSPEL ARTIST

BEGINNING THE PERMISSION JOURNEY

GOD MADE ME PRECISELY THE WAY HE DESIRED ME TO BE.

Realizing this was the single, monumental truth that changed everything in my life. It gave me permission to be exactly who God wanted me to be. To own the permission granted by my Creator. I heard His voice in my spirit affirming, "Jackie, I could have made you any way I wanted you. I made you precisely the way I desired."

And God also made you precisely the way He desired you to be.

Imagine a master artisan, carefully crafting a one-of-a-kind-in-all-the-world creation. That artist works with precision to ensure that the creation is exactly as he or she intends. And when the creation has been executed to perfection, it has immeasurable value and worth.

It's not accidental.

It's not haphazard.

It's *not flawed*.

Any altered version of you or me is counterfeit. And when

I use the word "counterfeit," I'm describing our behavior, our choices, the way we present ourselves that's not fully in line with *all* of who God made us to be.

When God dropped this insight on me, about His intentionality in our design, it triggered a deep dissatisfaction with a Jackie who was anything other than who God made me to be. Again and again this sacred awareness motivated me to lean into my commitment to be only who God made me to be. It allowed me to enjoy freedom!

This new revelation gave me permission to stop striving.

Permission to not change who I am.

Permission to not settle.

Permission to start right where I was.

Permission to shake off paralyzing fear.

Permission to show up as the bold woman I was created to be.

This insight gave me a hunger and passion to continue being the precise version that God designed.

And it's why I want to warn you not to get too comfortable. Not to accept the bondage of fear. Not to wither under your old wounds. Not to be bullied by the opinions of others. Not to make any excuse for not living in your God-given identity.

But many of us never pause to notice if we're actually living in freedom. And when we don't make time to stop and look at our lives, we remain stuck in bondage. We're hindered from living in the fullness of who we've been created to be. We live small because we don't even recognize that we're caged.

But as I meditated on what it looks like to live a life of

what I'm calling "permission," God showed me a picture of a captured lioness—one who was once free—being released back onto the spacious savannas and open grasslands where she once thrived. As she rejoins her pride, she realizes she is no longer bound. As she inhales fresh air, she stretches her strong legs and runs free. She is liberated to be who she was made to be.

And that's us! When we live with permission, we flourish as we breathe in the truth about who God says we are. We're released from the confines that have kept us bound. We break free from our shackles and cages to live in the fullness of who God created us to be.

This message of permission that I received from God, as well as an awareness of His love for women who aren't yet free, is what motivates me to show up daily in the fullness of who He made me to be. And I continue to be amazed at what God has done, and continues to do, through the permission movement that my team and I call the permission banner. As we're seeing women living in freedom, their lives looking vastly different from their peers', we are marveling at what God has done and continues to do.

Today countless women are finding freedom under the permission banner. In the virtual Permission World community, women are daily encouraging one another to live free. Inside our mentorship program, Permission Room, women are discovering how to experience intimacy with the Lord and how to live their lives in obedience to Him. And the *Permission Talk* podcast is meeting women right where they are and pushing them into purpose. Under the permission banner, every woman who desires to fight for her freedom is welcome. We've seen women from around the globe accept this invitation into freedom and gather at our Permission Conferences to worship and seek God together. This same freedom is available to you.

If you were to set this book down and look in the mirror, you'd see the version of yourself that you are in this moment. Take an honest look and really notice because this is your starting point! You don't start the journey from where you were two years ago. And you certainly don't start from where you hope to be tomorrow. You start where you are. Right now. As you are. And if you feel as if something is missing in today's version of you, let that motivate you on this journey to becoming the fullness of who God made you to be.

I am convinced that the message of permission has the power to change your life. I know because it changed my life and the lives of thousands of ladies who have learned to live free under the permission banner. This good news can deliver you from the bondage of settling. It can plant in you a hunger for more. It will ignite a discontentment with any identity other than the one God gave you when He made you. I want to equip you with a commitment to be the full version of who God made you to be in every room you enter!

Wherever you are today, there's more for you. There's more for you to experience. There's more for you to accomplish. If you still have breath, there's still more that the Father is desiring to unlock. It's already waiting inside of you, and God is in the process of birthing the truest version of who you were created to be.

She is fully free.

She is fully alive.

She is fully authentic.

Can you see her? Ask God to give you a glimpse of what she looks like. What she sounds like. How she behaves. How she takes up space. How she relates to others. But most important, how she relates to God. This is the woman who lives with permission, and she's waiting for you to discover her. This is the journey God is inviting you into.

Keep in mind, it's a lifelong process from which you never graduate. From now until Jesus returns, we will continuously be conformed more into this precise image that ultimately reflects the true nature of the Father. In this process we begin to look, respond, behave, and talk like Him! In the beginning He made an image bearer, created to reflect the likeness of the only perfect One. He arrays us with these attributes of Himself and makes us all unique to accomplish His good pleasure.

You deserve to discover and live in the fullness of who you were made to be. This is the life of freedom! I'm with you on this journey, and I'm rooting for you.

LOVE,
DR. JACKIE

ONE

PERMISSION TO BE
AUTHENTIC

For you created my inmost being; you knit
me together in my mother's womb.

PSALM 139:13

STEPPING TOWARD THE MUFFLED BUZZ OF WOMEN'S VOICES, I pulled back the black curtain to take a peek at the room. There wasn't one empty seat in the auditorium. And I knew thousands more were watching online, eager to hear a word from God that would grant them freedom. The space, both inside and out, had been carefully designed and decorated in a lush pink-and-green floral theme. Onstage, musicians and vocalists waited for their cue to begin worship. Pivoting, I slipped back to my office to do my final makeup touches in front of a well-lit mirror.

As I sat in my swivel chair I traced, with my favorite red lipstick, the curve of the lips God sculpted just for me.

I smiled.

When I looked in the mirror, the Jackie I saw was the Jackie who God has *always* seen—even when I didn't yet know her and couldn't yet see her. The face I saw in the mirror wasn't the four-year-old girl whose father returned to his homeland of Ghana—without her—to fulfill his mission to serve people there. She wasn't the girl who lived for years with the pain of so many unanswered questions regarding her father's departure: *Doesn't he love me? Are the people in Ghana more important than my brother and me? Why didn't we just go with him? Weren't we good enough for him to stay?* I didn't see that little girl who felt abandoned.

The reflection looking back at me wasn't that of grade school Jackie—the girl whose mother, in an attempt to tame her tight curls, mixed two chemicals that caused damage to more than her hair. The bald spots on her head were the only thing people could see. But on the inside the pain and embarrassment of being laughed at taught young Jackie that her hair wasn't good enough. That lie morphed into believing that *she* wasn't good enough. I didn't see that Jackie who felt ashamed.

When I looked in the mirror that night I didn't see the teenaged Jackie, who dressed to be accepted by the popular crowd at school. Who chauffeured her friends around. Who handed over her virginity because she felt it was expected of her. I didn't see the Jackie who sought to please others at her own expense. I didn't see that version of Jackie who was afraid.

I didn't see the dental student who worked so hard to make the grade. I didn't see the young woman who hustled to prove to her professors, prove to her parents, prove to herself that she was worthy. I didn't see that Jackie who felt insecure.

The woman I saw in the mirror's reflection wasn't even the Jackie of just five years earlier, who was launching a new church with her husband, Travis. That Jackie shined on the outside but privately felt isolated and insignificant. She longed to live a life of significance but felt paralyzed.

Instead, in my reflection I noticed a spot of lipstick on my tooth and wiped it away. Drawing a deep breath to calm my nerves, I felt excited for the evening. As I noticed, with fresh eyes, the woman God had always seen, I also heard His voice assuring me of the truth.

Jackie, lean on Me.

You're made in My image.

You carry My DNA.

You have dominion here.

You can do it.

It was the reliable voice, speaking the truth about who I am and who I've been made to be, the voice that had been growing louder and easier to recognize in my ear each day. It was *truth* that had been dripping into my deep and wounded places.

In the face of the woman in the mirror I *did* recognize the eager, feisty, inspired girl I used to be. I saw the four-year-old Jackie dressed in her church clothes, wearing Mama's long earrings. The ones with the little hearts with clear crystals. This little girl stood up in worship and proclaimed how good God was. She had big faith packed into a little girl body. Confident that she could believe God for anything, she testified, "God can heal my head!" "God can help me make a one hundred!" "God can make a way!" Before she felt shame, before she was wounded, four-year-old Jackie was *free.*

That was who God had always seen when He looked at me. And now, at last, I saw her too.

Glancing up, I saw a young woman standing at my door wearing a headset and carrying a clipboard. She let me know I had five minutes before they needed me backstage.

As the countdown continued, and I walked backstage, I

couldn't help but notice that my shiny patent leather boots, paired with my bright silver bubble pants and custom, floor-length fuchsia-pink bomber jacket, were a bold statement of who I was in that moment. I gave a quiet nod to that little girl in me who was still free to run, and skip, and jump, and dance.

When my assistant handed me the microphone before I stepped onstage, a moment I'd once experienced—very similar to this one—flooded through me with a force that surprised me. For now I'll just say that when I'd held the same microphone five years earlier, I had lost my voice. But *this* Jackie? The one I'd just seen in the mirror? The one God had always seen? She was fierce! She had things to say! And she was going to say them with *lots of volume*!

Stepping into the center-stage spotlight, I saw that spread out before me was a room full of royalty. God had designed these queens, from every walk of life, to be made fully alive.

"Welcome to the Permission Conference!" I announced with boldness.

If I could snap a photo of the Jackie that God had in mind from the very beginning, when He conceived of me, I'd take the image at that exact moment. Holding that microphone, standing in the presence of sisters who were as eager to receive from God as I was, I felt fully alive. Knowing the goodness that God had in store for those women, I was as aware of God's presence, around me and in me, as I'd ever been.

In that hour, I was the Jackie I was created to be.

For a variety of reasons, which I'll be sharing with you in these pages, *that* was my moment. And Sis, the reason I even mention *my* moment is because I know that your moment is coming. If God could transform me from the girl who felt shame and fear, God can transform you. I'm sure of it.

That's the good news.

But there's more to the story. Although God has always been the master designer of who I will become, it is a joint project. God has this good plan for my life, but there have been choices on the journey. And if I hadn't made those choices, if I hadn't said yes to God when I was given the opportunity, a thousand women in the room that night would not have heard what they needed to hear about God's good plan for them.

It makes me wonder: *Who's in the room where God has called you?* Who's waiting for you to walk in and offer the gifts that you've been given? It may not be a sanctuary or an auditorium. Maybe it's a nursery. Or it's the bleachers at a Little League game. It might be a boardroom. It might be the hospital bedroom where your grandmother is preparing to meet Jesus.

As I think about that room where you're being called, and the people to whom you've been called, I also think about who it is that God has made you to be. I begin to imagine who your Creator has designed you to be, and I can't help but wonder who *you* saw when you looked in the mirror this morning.

Did you see the girl who suffered at the hands of someone who should have protected her? Did you see the little girl who went to bed hungry? Did you see the girl who was teased for being overweight? Or did you see the girl who used substances to numb herself from pain? If you're seeing *that* girl, it might feel like your moment will never come. I get it. A few years ago I would not have dreamed that I'd be living with the kind of freedom I enjoy today.

And that's why it's so important for you to hear that I believe your moment is coming.

If that scares you a little bit, if you feel afraid when you think of discovering and stepping into the big purpose God has for you, I completely understand. That was my story! But I also know that God equips you to push through that fear to become exactly who He made you to be. This is what He required of me as well.

Although I wouldn't have chosen to experience everything I went through in my past, I'm convinced that none of it has been wasted. What I faced didn't break me; it *made* me. And God will use everything you have faced for the purpose He has for your life. Throughout these pages I'll be encouraging you to own these areas of your life where your security fails. Where you're striving. Where you're not living authentically. The areas where you're still hiding. Where you've refused to take off the mask. *God can't heal what we hide!* This book is your opportunity to dig deep to find out what's really at your core. God isn't intimidated by what we find. *He just desires access!* I am a living witness that He is faithful. *God will heal what we are brave enough to expose.* You will see this become more apparent as we move forward together.

And as you consider the places in your life that God wants to redeem, those areas where you're not yet living authentically, I want to encourage you to think about them in three ways. When you're not being who God made you to be, you're likely living as (1) less than, (2) more than, or (3) other than who God made you to be.

When you fail to fully use what God has given—your gifts, talents, passions, wiring—for the sake of others, you're being *less than* who God made you to be. When you pose, by trying to impress with your status or appearance or belongings, you're behaving as if you're *more than* who God made you to be. And when you try to imitate others, you're being *other than* who God made you to be. We all have room to grow in living with more permission, and the call I'm issuing in these pages invites you into that transformation. If you're not yet living authentically, ask God to show you which of these three tendencies might be your particular temptation.

Along the way I'll be sharing my story and what freedom has looked like in my life. Maybe through this book you're meeting me for the first time. I want you to make sure that you see the real picture of who I am because Instagram feeds and google searches show only the *highlights*. They leave out the low moments. They showcase pretty pictures and fancy words, but I want to show you the fullness of my journey. I want to show you those low moments, when I was desperate before the Lord, seeking my purpose. I've learned that those other first impressions—based on degrees, titles, staged photo shoots, and how polished things look on the outside—will always tell an incomplete story. I want every woman who holds this book to realize that we are all just girls who have gathered the courage to become the women God made us to be.

It can be tempting to believe that we'll never own our true essence. I'm sure many of you can relate. I know exactly what this is like, because on any given day I might feel like the confident version of my authentic self, but it's also possible that I'll wake up feeling like the not-yet-there version. Thankfully, what I have gained in my understanding of permission helps me feel like the confident version 90 percent of the time.

But those other days? When I wake up not feelin' like the Jackie God made me to be, I have to *choose* to be the real Jackie. When I look in the mirror and see fearful Jackie, or the Jackie who's striving to be worthy, I make the choice to see who God sees. To not give in to what I feel but instead live in the truth. I remind myself of who I really am.

And that's why I have such a passion to be raw and transparent with you about what it looks like to live out the permission granted by God. If you're feeling like there is no hope for you to become a more anchored version of yourself, my heart aches for you. Or maybe you're that woman who feels as if you have it all, but you're not living in a rich, intimate, dependent relationship with the Lord. Sis, I need you to hear that God has so much more in store for you to become.

If you have a sense that God is inviting you to become who He designed you to be, I hope you'll continue with me. If you're ready to be honest, I want you to step into this ever-evolving adventure to become all that God has desired you to be from the moment He formed you.

As I share what this process has looked like in my life, I want to open the doors wide to the various stages and phases of growing in ownership of permission. I'm going to share the tools and revelations that have helped me in this walk and help me partner with you over the long haul.

When you wake up tomorrow morning, I want you to look in the mirror and notice who you see. Maybe you *will* see the girl who was sad, or mad, or afraid. Let her know that you see her, and you care. Assure her that you're here for her. And then welcome God to show you who He sees when He looks at you. Ask Him to reveal the unique purpose He has for you that only you can fulfill. And invite Him to show you the people—who you may already know and love—who are waiting for you to take center stage. Who are ready for you to pick up the microphone, or the clipboard, or the scalpel, or the teddy bear, or the gavel. Sister, God is going to do it! He's going to show you who He designed you to be. He's going to reveal your purpose. And He's going to lead you toward the ones who are waiting for you.

You ready for this? Now is the moment you begin. And here is the place where God will begin to inspire you, equip you, and send you.

You were made for this.

You were made to live fully and authentically.

You were made for freedom.

══ **Embrace Permission Exercise** ══

1. When you look in the mirror, who do you see?
2. As you look back on your life, reflect on who you used to be when you were younger and less mature. How does she compare to who you are today?
3. This week, grab a notebook or a journal and spend some time writing and reflecting on your life. This may lead to a moment of celebration or an awareness of an area that the Father still desires to touch.

══ **Prayer** ══

Let's pray together.

Daddy, I believe that You are doing a new thing in me today. Help me to see what You have already been doing in my life and open my heart to receive the freedom You have in store. I want to be the unique woman You have created and gifted me to be, and I'm ready to be transformed. In Jesus' name, amen.

TWO

PERMISSION TO WAKE UP

Open my eyes to see the wonderful
truths in your instructions.

PSALM 119:18 (NLT)

I WAS FROZEN IN FEAR.

Buckled securely in my Ford Mustang convertible, I had just been jolted awake to find my car rapidly heading off the highway. Instinctively, I gripped the steering wheel as my car lifted off the road and spun through the air. Sky and earth rotated past me as I rolled with the vehicle. After flipping three times, my car finally landed upright about fifteen yards from where it had launched off the quiet country road in the wee hours of the morning.

One night when I was in high school my mom, a pharmacist, was working the night shift. We lived in the country and my brother, who was a senior at the time, was staying with a friend in town. Without my mother's knowledge or permission, I'd gone to pick up my boyfriend, Lance, so that we could spend time together. We were on our way back to my house, on dark country roads where deer would often dash into traffic at night. Lance decided that it would be funny to shut off the lights to my car and drive down these long, winding, deer-filled roads in the pitch black. To say that I became furious is an understatement.

By the time we made it to my house, I was completely over even being near Lance. I left him out in the living room, went into my room, and began to clean. It was already late at this point, and I was so irritated. I kept asking him to let me take him back home, but he refused to leave. As soon as I got my room exactly the way I wanted it, he came in and started to throw things off my dresser onto the floor. He knocked all the pillows off my bed and unmade my bed. At this point, I made him get his things so I could take him home.

It was around midnight when we headed to his house. I was so sleepy that I was having a hard time keeping my eyes open. We didn't utter one word to each other the whole twenty-five-minute drive. Even as he got out of the car, it was completely silent. I didn't even care that he slammed the door as he left, I was just so glad to see him go. I chose a route home where the highway was undergoing construction. Trying desperately to stay alert, I continued to doze off and wake up.

Suddenly I awoke and braced myself as my car was about to hit one of the large orange construction cones. But rather than skidding into a cone, I flew off the road at the *one area* along this whole highway that wasn't lined with large boulders and cement blocks. Tumbling down a steep embankment, flipping through the air, I felt as if the terror was never going to end. The car finally landed, and I was so grateful to be alive.

It was freezing cold, and I was so afraid. My mom had just bought me that car less than two weeks earlier, and now it was destroyed. There was glass everywhere, and all hopes of finding my phone faded as I continued to cut my hand looking for it. I kicked the rest of the glass out of my driver's side window and climbed out of the wreckage.

Because the area was so rural, the houses were very far apart. There was no traffic on the road in the middle of the night, so I began walking to find help. The first house I reached had a large Beware of Dogs sign as well as one saying No Trespassing. I quickly decided that it was way too dark to take any more chances. Having survived the wreck, there was no way I would risk being eaten by dogs.

The only option I had left was to continue walking until I got to another house. Touching my ear and noticing blood on my finger, I automatically began thinking the worst and assumed I was bleeding internally. Terrified, embarrassed, and full of shame, I tortured myself with words of how worthless I was and how dishonorable a daughter I must be to betray my mother's trust when she'd given everything for my brother and me.

When I finally arrived at the next house, about half a mile down the road, a couple came to the door. Alarmed and concerned, they welcomed me into their home and called an ambulance and the police as I cried uncontrollably.

After they called the police, my first call was to my mom. Hearing her calm, soothing voice, I relaxed a bit. She called my aunt Janise to come get me after the EMS workers confirmed that I was okay. That night I walked away from an accident that could have killed me. All I had was a small scratch on my leg. I must have touched that scratch before touching my ear.

The next morning I told my mom that I'd been hungry and wanted cereal, so I had driven to a store to get some milk.

She and I have always had a very close relationship, and—until then—I had always been honest with her. So, assuming I had no reason to lie to her, she believed me.

A few months later my brother, Norman, somewhat jokingly asked me, "Jackie, that night you had the wreck, what really happened?"

Initially I played it cool, recounting to him the story I had told everyone else. In the middle of this rendition, though, something made me feel that it was safe to tell Norman the whole story. Of course, my disclosure came after demanding one hundred promises that he wouldn't say anything. He broke that promise when he went and spilled the news to my mom.

When Norman told her, he made her promise that she wouldn't come straight to me about it. And she honored his wishes. She kept his secret. A few weeks later something about the wreck came up, and I felt this burden to tell my mom the truth.

Before telling her the real story, I begged her not to be mad at me. To her credit, she responded well.

"Jackie," she gently asked, "why didn't you think that you could tell me the truth from the beginning?"

Of course, that wasn't about *her* as much as it was about *me*. I was ashamed that I'd had Lance over. And her kindness made me feel even more horrible. As we continued to talk, I promised her that I would never lie to her again.

Sometimes it takes hitting rock bottom to recognize that you are worth too much to settle.

WAKING UP

A literal crash caused me to wake up and look at my life. In the journey from being stuck to living free, God's Holy Spirit wakes us up. Sometimes, as with my car accident, it's a loud, blaring, alarm-clock kind of wake-up. And other times, the Spirit will nudge us more gently, opening our eyes to where we are stuck and quickening our hearts with a passion to live free.

Sis, God is never content to let us stay stuck in the counterfeit life. So the Spirit is always offering us permission to step into freedom. And whether it's the rude alarm clock awakening of a crash—an accident, a diagnosis, a divorce, another sudden rupture—or the more gentle nudging of God's call, God is calling *you*.

During these pivotal moments and seasons, whether sudden or slow, God invites us to wake up to what matters most in life. These seasons or moments can also divide our lives into *before* and *after*.

Before we wake up, we may be cruising through life. We might be living at the height of success, and we don't want to be slowed down. We get in a routine that numbs us to noticing what's around us. We don't recognize where we really are.

The beauty and gift of transitional moments, however, is that they slow us down. They give us an opportunity to collect ourselves, take stock, figure things out. And when we choose to seize that opportunity, we have the chance to participate in what happens in the *after* part of our stories.

⚷━•-0   **Prayer Prompt**

God, as I look at my life, show me the moment or moments when You were giving me an opportunity to wake up to live anew for You. *(That moment may be right now!)*

MY MOM'S TRANSITION

I saw this pivotal metamorphosis happen later in my mother's life. For her, and for many, it wasn't a car crash. It was retirement. It was her opportunity to look at how she had been living and how she *could* be living.

While she was working for decades as a pharmacist, my mom was somewhat isolated. She didn't grab lunch with girlfriends. She rarely did anything outside of her normal routine. And she limited her level of influence to just a few people she encountered daily. She lived a lot of her life for Norman and me versus in full obedience to all that God desired of her. She definitely *loved* God, but for a host of reasons her job and her family were what she was living for.

I think her life was like a lot of women's lives. We never intend to forsake the fullness of all God has for us or live inauthentic lives, but there are all these influences that keep us from digging deep and living from that foundational core of who we are: God's beloved daughters. A lot of us get caught up in doing good things, but because we're always in motion we never stop to ask God how we've been uniquely designed to do the thing that only we can do.

When my mom paused to take that assessment of her life, as she moved into retirement, she caught a glimpse of what God was calling her to be. She chose to step into a life that was much richer and fuller than the one she'd been living.

Today, she's active in church.

She's investing in friendships.

She's pouring her life into mentoring women from around the world.

She's very present as a grandma to her grandchildren.

She uses her voice more.

She grabs dinner with women from church.

And she made the decision to go back to school to study counseling in response to the invitation to be *all* that God had called her to be. When she retired, a shift in financial circumstances also taught her to trust in God's provision in brand-new ways. When this happens in these transitional moments—both the ones we choose and the ones that choose us—the Lord shows Himself to us in new ways.

> ### *You Are God's Daughter.*
> See what great love the Father has lavished on us, that we should be called children of God! And that is what we are!
> —1 JOHN 3:1

In my mom's case, it gave her a fresh vision of her provider, Jehovah Jireh. She was comfortable for years as a pharmacist, and a part of her believed that she was responsible for her provision. That's real, isn't it? It's so easy to lose sight of the truth we know. But when she was no longer pouring her life into her family and job, her eyes were opened to see that the job was never actually the thing providing for her. It had *always* been God.

I hope you can see through my mom's story that it's never too late to begin the permission journey! Wherever you are in your walk with God today, He is inviting you to take that first step.

AWAKENED BY PAIN

God is all about waking us up to the reality of who we are and the greater reality of who we are in Him. Sometimes that awakening will happen, as it did for my mom, when we enter a new season of life. Other times it will be because our old wounds are throbbing. God will open our eyes to the ways we've been bullied by the opinions of others. Life just stops working for us, and we become desperate for God's help.

Today you may not be where you want to be—in your life with God, in your relationships with family and friends, or in the way you're living out your unique purpose. And that's okay. It's okay to be where you are today because God knows exactly where you are! He doesn't expect you to be someplace else. Or someone else. I want you to be able to offer yourself grace in this moment. As women we can be quick to offer acceptance and compassion to others but fail to extend the same to ourselves. And the voice in our head begins to lie to us . . .

This hurts too much.

I shouldn't be dealing with this still.

I'm never going to change.

God can't handle this.

I'm supposed to be better than this.

Sis, I want you to hear God saying, "No, no, no, no, baby. Just as you are." If you're broken. If you're addicted. If you're undone. Whatever you're facing, God is present. And He welcomes you to share the hurts, the pains, the fears. Whatever you're experiencing.

First, if you're stinging from past hurts, or even fresh emotional wounds, *accept* where you are so that you can move forward.

Second, *avail* yourself of the resources God provides to help you heal. God is so faithful to pro-

God Is With You.

Since you are precious and honored in my sight, and because I love you, I will give people in exchange for you. . . . Do not be afraid, for I am with you.

—Isaiah 43:4–5

vide trained professionals to walk with you through trauma. Through addiction. Through depression. Through anxiety. These servants can offer you practical tools to navigate your healing. The key is that you have to be honest about where you are. That's why twelve-step meetings begin with introductions: "I'm Sandra and I'm an alcoholic." That's the posture we need to have with God. "I'm Carrie, and I've been sexually abused." "I'm Tamika, and I've been wounded in this place." That posture of honesty opens the door for God's healing.

You might need to speak to a licensed professional. You might need to share with a trusted friend. You might need to find the right community, whether a friend group or church home. We don't walk the healing journey alone; we do it with others.

IT'S TIME TO TELL THE TRUTH

As you are waking up to where you are today, are you identifying a wound you've been carrying with you? Are you noticing the ways that you appear and behave to please others? While this may feel disheartening, understand that you are in the *perfect place*. Because the kind of honesty that allows you to see what's true about you is pivotal to your healing journey!

For example, maybe you've always told yourself, "Yes, I'm adopted, but that just means that there are lots of people who love me." But now God is showing you that you've been hauling around a wound of rejection.

Or you've always insisted, "I only wear extensions because they're convenient." But the Spirit is showing you that you wear them because you've been unconsciously believing that it's the only way you'll feel attractive.

Perhaps you say, "I wear these clothes that highlight my curves because I love fashion." But maybe God is showing you that your value isn't contingent on men finding you physically attractive.

New opportunities call and you find every reason in your schedule to say they can't work, because you're not sure *you* will work in a new opportunity.

It's easy for you to show up, love, pray for, and diagnose everyone else, but this has a lot to do with the fact that you truly hate being alone to look at *you*. So you decide to just be savior for everyone else, to push everyone else forward.

You insist that you're available to all people at all times because that's what a good friend or pastor does, but it has a lot to do with you believing that if they can't reach you, then God won't be enough for them.

Maybe you continuously emphasize supporting your husband and your children. But the truth is that it's not just about support—it has a lot to do with your fear of stepping out into the new thing God is saying to do.

When you begin to hear God's gentle voice whispering what is most true, listen. If you don't face the truth, you'll never get healed.

Women who know me well know that I shout this message from the mountaintops! And the reason I'm so passionate about it is because I used to be stuck in the same lies—that I wasn't good enough the way God made me, that I had to prove myself, etc. And I was paralyzed by those lies.

If you're not willing to face the truth, you won't get healed. It's like going to the doctor sick and insisting that you're well. You'll never get the help you need if you insist on believing the lie that you couldn't be healthier than you are right now. Yet when you unlock the door of honesty, you're finally positioned to receive all that God has for you.

For me, that door of honesty had the word "hair" carved into it. Due to that painful hair experience I endured as a girl, I lived most of my life feeling as if my hair could never be good enough. Hiding it was a much easier way to cope. It helped me avoid the truth of my pain and brokenness.

> ### God's Truth Sets You Free.
>
> To the Jews who had believed him, Jesus said, "If you hold to my teaching, you are really my disciples. Then you will know the truth, and the truth will set you free."
> —John 8:31–32

"Jackie," I heard God whisper to me, "you don't wear those extensions because they're easy. You do it because it makes you feel more beautiful." Without that truth, I would never have gotten to the point with God where I truly believed that the way I was made was beautiful. That the true essence of my being was beautiful.

Sure, I'd heard people say I was beautiful. (My mom. My husband. That's what they are supposed to say.) When people tried to convince and assure me that I was attractive, their approval was never enough because a louder voice in my head knew what traits the world valued. Ultimately, I had to hear from *God*, not people.

This is why honesty is the first step to a beautiful life of freedom. It sounds so simple, and in some ways it is simple. But you have to exercise the courage to face the truth and own it. It may be hard, even strange at first, but the more you embrace a life of honesty, the more natural it becomes.

THE LIE CAN BE SUBTLE

It's important that you hear that the lie can be very indistinct. If it were big and blatant—"You're an ugly monster!"—we'd catch it, right? But the lie that has its grip on us is more subtle. We twist the truth a little bit to suit ourselves. In my life it sounded like, "Sure, I know I'm beautiful. But I just think these extensions are convenient. Or this weave means I have less to manage." It sounds true, but when I got honest with myself, I heard the lie that was cleverly woven in: "You're not quite good enough as you are." Man, this was a hard pill of truth to swallow, but I'm grateful I did!

As a college student driving myself into a state of exhaustion from overwork, I insisted, "I just want to be sure that everything I do is excellent." But if I was honest, I'd have to admit how important it was to me that people knew I was smart. That I was enough. I sacrificed relationships and fellowship to get straight As—and that one B—so that my final GPA was 3.96. But guess what? Those are just three numerals that do not define anyone's worth.

If we've taken a vow of celibacy and end up sleeping with a boyfriend, we'll reason, "I just want him to know I'm his ride or die. I just want to show him I love him." When, if we're honest with ourselves, we might discover that we slept with him because we were scared that if we didn't, he'd leave.

We lie to ourselves a lot.

I'll tell myself, "I'm being this over-the-top mom to ensure that these boys will be the best they can be." Really? When I finally got honest, I was able to admit that the boys having the best was a part of the truth, but not *all* the truth. I also wanted people to know I was a great mom. My own uncertainty about whether I was enough was a driving factor, not just the well-being of my boys.

One of the big problems about believing the enemy's lies or being bullied by half-truths is that it keeps us from living out our unique purpose. God has work for us to do—custom fit to how we are made! When we get tangled up believing the enemy's lie, we're sidetracked from doing the thing for which God designed us. That kingdom assignment that *only* we can do.

The lie the enemy uses to trick us isn't always easy to notice. We believe that because a lie has some truth, it is not a lie. But if something is not fully true, it's not truth. To be healed and live with permission, you have to go after the whole truth and nothing but the truth! And that's exactly what God's Spirit does by opening our eyes and ears to recognize the lie about our identity that's keeping us stuck. In a little letter in the back of the New Testament, called 1 John, we're reminded, "God is light; in him there is no darkness at all" (1 John 1:5). When you have believed a lie, you can be confident that God will shine light into that darkness, opening your eyes to what is most true.

The problem is that when we don't face what's most true, when we live with that subtle lie, we'll find ways to blame others—even when the problem lies inside us.

So you blame your husband, who's not supporting you.

You blame your mama, who pushed you too hard.

You blame the teacher, who didn't prepare you for the test.

> *You Are Unique and You Were Made for a Unique Purpose.*
>
> For we are God's handiwork, created in Christ Jesus to do good works, which God prepared in advance for us to do.
> —EPHESIANS 2:10

But when you have the courage to look inside, you'll finally discover what's really holding you back.

WELCOME TO THE NEW

If you've been in a car crash, you know that there are those moments after impact where you are trying to regain your bearings. You begin to notice the reality of where you are: shattered glass, bulging airbags, bent metal. And you take stock of limbs and organs to determine if you, or anyone else, has sustained injuries.

Was there a moment like that in your life? Perhaps in the

recent past or maybe in the present? You may have felt bruised and bloodied. Disoriented. You may have paused to take stock of your life. I want you to notice that in that moment you were not alone. You are loved by God, and the Father who loves you was present with you. Even if you weren't aware of His presence in that moment, can you see Him now? His arms are embracing you. And then, as they release, they point you into a new future. And He stays with you to navigate the journey. When you fear the future you can't yet see, He's with you to guide you. And maybe this book is the map to guide you into your own awakening.

You Are Loved by Jesus.

As the Father has loved me, so have I loved you. Now remain in my love.
—John 15:9

Remember what changed my life? My car crash on a dark country road was a wake-up call for me. It opened my eyes to the fact that I wasn't being who God made me to be. Even though I didn't yet understand the big, beautiful promise of permission living—of being fully and precisely who God made me to be— God was already showing me that I was made for more.

I hope that you don't have to have a life-threatening accident to wake up to this moment of your life. And God is so wonderfully creative that He can wake us up in so many ways.

Maybe your wake-up will be gentler than mine. You recognize a growing dissatisfaction with the life you've been living. Even if you can't quite put your finger on it, you begin to sense that somewhere, somehow, some way there is more for you in this life.

Maybe a trusted friend comes to you and gently says, "Hey girl, you know I love you, right? And right now, I don't recognize you. What's going on?"

Or it might be bad news. A jarring diagnosis. The death of a loved one. The announcement that your spouse is leaving. The loss of a home.

Beloved, is God nudging you awake today? Is He calling your name? Is He inviting you to discover how He sees you and be transformed by that truth?

Sis, don't resist!

Don't hit the snooze button.

God is after you.

The moment is now.

Let's do this.

═══ **Embrace Permission Exercise** ═══

God is faithful to wake us up to what He has for us.

1. How has God woken you up? Was it a crash, like mine? Was it a season of transition? Was it a difficult challenge or loss you faced?
2. *Today*, what is God showing you about yourself?
3. What in this chapter helped you notice and connect with the way God is waking you up?

Prayer ═

Let's pray together.

Lord, I confess that I have not yet become all that You created me to be. Wake me up! Open my eyes to notice where I've been and discern where You are calling me. Reveal any subtle lies that I've embraced. I offer my whole life to You because I am ready to be who You designed me to be. In Jesus' name, amen.

THREE

PERMISSION TO NOTICE WHERE YOU'RE STUCK

*The thief comes only to steal and kill and destroy; I have
come that they may have life, and have it to the full.*

JOHN 10:10

"HEY, BABE," TRAVIS SPOKE IN MY EAR AS WE PREPARED FOR worship at the church we were starting in Columbia, South Carolina, "I'm going to have you do the welcome tonight after we end worship."

He might as well have told me to preach my first sermon.

I had met Travis my sophomore year of college when he returned to be part of a worship event on campus. I had never encountered a man that young demonstrating the power of God at that level. I was blown away by his commitment to obey God above his own agenda. I loved how radical and unapologetic his love for God was. He alluded to his previous reputation being that of a frat boy who ran the yard, but to watch his passion for seeing the lives of his peers set free, you could tell that the previous reputation meant nothing to him. He laid it down with ease for a much greater call. He was on fire, and I loved it! His worship, smile, and personality were all captivating. I had never encountered a person like him before.

What began with Travis's weak attempt at flirting in a parking lot after a campus event morphed into a friendship that became more. He was a true man of God—one whom I would not even kiss for the first three years we dated. We had the same values, morals, and ambitions. He was an absolute breath of fresh air.

I will spare you the bumps in our relationship, but *trust*: we faced them. We both still had a lot of growing to do (more him than me!) from the night we met till the time we decided we were going to put in the work to be in a steady relationship.

But back to Travis making this nonchalant request for me to do the welcome . . .

If you're a woman who enjoys the spotlight and are confident that God has given you something to say, you'd love that opportunity! But in that moment it absolutely terrified me.

Back in 2016 we'd begun our Monday night Worship and Word services downtown at a venue called Agape. Our first service was so intimate and powerful. We'd been there only about three months, and in that time we had to expand twice within that building to hold all the people who began consistently showing up.

Moments before we began our very first service, Travis walked up and asked me to do the welcome. After the invitation he just kept on moving to the next thing on his to-do list.

I knew his request was harmless. It would be such an easy thing for him to pull off with no preparation. I knew he wanted to share the spotlight so that our new church family would get to know us both. And he believed in me so much!

I knew how much time and energy we'd both put into preparing for the service. I knew I wanted to—and would—do anything I could to support him. But at that time, being naked and vulnerable in front of people, pulling words out of thin air, wasn't in my skill set. Not in public settings! Travis was the public speaker: the man was made for the spotlight. I was happy to be in the background, and he knew that about me.

So the question stuck in my head was, *What is he thinking?* He knew all his famous friends who'd joined us that evening would be watching, and one was even sitting on the front row. I didn't want to embarrass him or make a fool of myself. Travis is spontaneous and speaks off the cuff; I need to prepare, and I didn't have any prep time. I was way out of my comfort zone.

I was shaken up but, wanting to please, I agreed.

My mama has always been a voice who helps center me and bring me back to peace. The moment I saw her come through the doors that Monday evening, I ran in her direction. Just as the worship team was getting ready to begin, I grabbed her and went into a room to cry. Through tears I told her that I didn't feel ready to say a welcome. I was crying profusely, mainly because I was disappointed in myself for feeling the way I did in that moment.

As God was using us to birth a new church, I said things to myself like, "Jackie, how are you going to have Travis calling you a lead co-pastor, and you can't even get up and say a welcome! You are literally a doctor, and you can't even do a welcome! All your life people have spoken over and over about how much potential you have, but saying a welcome has you in a back room crying! What in the world are you going to do when God asks you to preach your first sermon?"

Mama's always been my greatest cheerleader and so patient with me. Her voice cut through all the tormenting thoughts as she began to pray God's Word over me. She wasn't moved by my tears or even my doubts. And after praying, my mom calmly encouraged, "Baby, just go out there and be who you are."

My mom has been a unique gift as I've sought to regain the permission granted to me by the Father. From season to season she's always shown me compassion and patience, all while remembering young girl Jackie. The girl that was sure of who she was in the Lord. Despite how I may have responded in a given moment, my mom was always sure of who I truly was. She never lost sight of that young girl who spoke with authority and lived from her heart back in her early days. And in that moment she was encouraging me to be the bold, uninhibited little girl who spoke her mind so easily when she was four years old, not caring what others thought.

What I knew about myself was that I was afraid to move forward in the purpose God had for me. I was afraid to speak. I was afraid I'd choke on my words. But God was nudging me, and I made the decision to go for it. I had agreed to speak, and I wasn't going to care what I sounded like. When God created me, He gave me permission to be all that I could be. That night I decided I was going to take God up on what He'd already given me. Permission.

ARE YOU STUCK?

From the outside, everything seemed fine. But internally I'd become okay with settling for this familiar version of myself and not going after more. It was comfortable, the safe version, and it looked good. It's important that you hear me: At one time in my life I was convinced that this version of me was good enough. But God, in His love, came to shake me and wake me up. He began to create a discomfort and burden in me to press for more. As God wakes us up to something new, we can respond in one of three ways.

First, we can agree to go on the journey toward newness. When we really believe that God has more for us, and when we're willing to walk with Him into what we can't yet see, we'll say yes to His invitation.

The second way we can respond is with a hard *no*. If we're scared of the journey ahead, we might simply and honestly tell God that we're not willing to take the risk of living in a new way.

And the third way, which a lot of us choose, is to stall. We deflect God's gracious invitation with an answer of "not now." If our lives are working well enough, if we're comfortable, we might choose to ignore God. If we don't yet have the vision to see the beautiful future that God sees, we might just drag our feet. And when we do, we miss out on the goodness He has for us. In some ways, that was my story. It looked like I had it all together, but what I didn't see or understand yet was how much I was leaving on the table by not pressing toward my *more*!

I want to pause here in case this or something similar is your story. Maybe you can't check off the same boxes I did, but your life, for the most part, is working. Your job is secure.

You're dating a pretty good guy. Or your marriage is good enough. The kids are fed and clothed. You serve at church. In some ways you're living on autopilot. You might not yet have everything you desire, but your life is pretty good.

If this is you, I need you to stick with me, because I'm about to introduce you to five women whose stories might be similar to yours. And while each of these women is getting by, not one of them is yet living the authentic version of who God created her to be. Kind of like me, that first service at Forward City.

It's so important for you to consider the profiles of five women on the pages to come because although they were getting by, *God had so much more for them.*

Did you hear that?

God had more for them.

And God has more for you.

What I know from experience is that when things are going well enough for us, it can dull our appetite for God's voice. We can often lose sight of what we still may be missing. Being comfortable creates a false security that everything is perfect! That we are at our optimum self. This causes us to live less than full lives. We might lose our desperation to hear God's leading. To receive from Him. To obey Him. To push, sacrifice, stretch, or get uncomfortable. Because in our desperate moments, when things are totally chaotic, we are all ears! We are primed and *ready* to receive what God has for us. But if you're checking all the boxes that say that you're comfortable, I am asking God to do something new in you.

And I'm asking Him to let you see what that is. *God, open their eyes to all the possibilities that a new yes can provide.*

As you meet these women, ask God to show you what He wants you to see *in yourself.* They exemplify five of the most common attributes I've seen that stifle women from owning the permission to live freely. I'm asking God's Spirit to show you which of these qualities are reflected in your own life. Each lady is stuck in some way. They're not bad. They're not broken. They're just *stuck.* Just like we can get stuck. In the various seasons of my journey with permission, I've identified with each one of these stories in some way. The good news is that as each lady became aware of where she was stuck, she had the opportunity to become free!

COMFORTABLE COURTNEY

First, I want to introduce you to Comfortable Courtney. She is a successful prosecuting attorney, and if you saw her walking through an airport or shopping at the mall, you'd think she has it all together. She has designer bags. She has the handsome, successful husband, two kids, and a dog. Twenty years ago she graduated at the top of her class from Harvard Law, passed the bar, and has been practicing law ever since.

Yet there is a pervasive dissatisfaction that gnaws at Courtney, and she can't quite put her finger on what it is. Though she has the degrees on the wall, the cars in the garage, and the hubby and kids in the big house, Courtney is still missing something. She hasn't yet realized that the accolades from law school are no longer fulfilling her. The family that looks great on the Christmas card every year can't meet her deeper needs.

There is more inside Courtney that needs to be discovered. There are gifts God has given her that need to be expressed. But she's settled. She's comfortable. She's coasting. She's allowed past success to quench her thirst for present and future purpose. There is a song in Courtney's heart that God is inviting her to sing, but because she's trusting in all she's achieved, she can't hear the invitation. That new song might be a literal song that needs to be composed and sung. It might be a mentoring program for women who haven't had the opportunities Courtney's had. It might be welcoming a foster child into her comfortable home. But Courtney won't receive all that God has for her until she pauses to listen to what God's voice is speaking to her *today*.

Courtney is comfortable and complacent.

Maybe you have a little bit of Courtney in you. Maybe you've settled into the grind and you're going through the motions of work, or school, or childcare. There's nothing particularly wrong with what you've got going, but you're on autopilot. Even if you're not comfortable financially, you find a certain comfort in your routine. And, without ever realizing it, you've stopped asking God what else He's calling you to do.

I get it, Sis. I do. But I also know that there is so much more for you. God has a plan and a purpose for you *today*.

Right now! *Don't allow past success to quench your thirst for present and future purpose.*

🗝️ **Prayer Prompt**

Father, I believe that You made me for so much more than comfort. Show me any area in my life where ease or convenience interferes with Your unique plan for me.

FEARFUL FRIEDA

The next woman I want you to meet is Fearful Frieda. Frieda is single and works as an accountant for a local builder. Like Courtney, there's so much more inside Frieda than she's living today.

Frieda's friends and church community have seen little glimpses of the fullness of who God made her to be. For example, on prayer retreats Frieda has moments of operating in a fiery freedom. She feels God working in her and through her, and the other women are blessed by what she shares. But on Monday morning, Frieda clams up, retreating into the shell she's used to wearing. There's a disconnect between the Frieda who's alive and on fire and the Frieda who's just getting by.

Frieda is bound by fear.

She's afraid her home isn't good enough. She's afraid she's not attractive enough. She's afraid to go after her dream job, sure it's out of reach. She's afraid to believe God for a husband and children. Frieda's afraid that she's not good enough, certain that other women—the ones with more degrees, or higher salaries, or more social media followers—are the ones that God blesses. Not her.

Frieda has always wanted to be a writer. But her default is to believe that she doesn't have what it takes. That she won't succeed. That others have the right gifts but that she does not. And when she sits down to write, a voice that lies whispers, "Who do you think you are? You don't have what it takes." And that fear that's bossing her around keeps Frieda bound.

Can you relate to Frieda's fears? Perhaps when you were a girl you had a dream of what you'd do with your life. But when that dream didn't magically unfold, you let it go. Fear kept you from going after it. Fear kept you stuck.

Sis, if you still have a memory of what that dream was that God put in your heart—to design, to lead, to perform, to teach—there is still time. If, after your failed relationships, you fear you'll never be chosen, never be seen as enough, there is *more*. God's plan for you is bigger than your fear. It's bigger than the obstacles before you. It's more abundant than you've dared to imagine. If fear has held you back, God has more for you, and in this moment He wants to push you forward. I've found that one of the greatest attacks on fear is to stand up and look it dead in the face. You have to face fear to beat fear!

Prayer Prompt

Daddy, I trust You, and I believe that Your perfect love casts out fear. Show me any area in my life where I am bound by fear.

TRAUMATIZED TAMMY

Tammy is a schoolteacher. And recently she's been suffering emotionally.

When she was a girl, a family member abused her. To protect herself from facing what was too much for a little girl to face, she buried what happened to her. She guarded her heart so that she wouldn't be hurt again. Tammy remembered what happened *cognitively*, but she had never faced the emotions of feeling unprotected as a little girl. She couldn't.

Tammy has trouble trusting others. Without realizing she was guarding herself from hurt, she's created a life for herself that's fairly isolated. She had a good group of girlfriends in college, but when one girl shared about her own abuse, Tammy ended the friendship. And she hasn't prioritized making friends with other women since then. Without fully realizing it, Tammy's doing her best to avoid situations that might lead her to confront the trauma she experienced. And while Tammy has had a few relationships with men, the childhood sexual abuse she endured causes her to leave before she becomes emotionally vulnerable.

45

For years, ignoring what happened worked. But recently old memories and feelings have been plaguing her. She's hurting and doesn't know how to *not hurt*.

The trauma Tammy endured is affecting her life in ways that she can't fully understand until she faces the past. When she finally does choose to do that hard work—in the presence of a therapist, pastor, prayer warrior, or other trusted friend—that healing will radically change her relationship with herself, others, and God. And then she can begin to rediscover the purpose that God has for her right now.

Maybe there's a hurt or trauma in your past that you've tried to ignore. Or maybe the impact of an old trauma is expressing itself in a new way in your life today. For instance, sometimes a new marriage or new child can unlock something we hadn't realized had a lasting impact on us. Maybe you love God, but because of the trauma of the past, you're struggling with anxiety and depression. Or you might be suffering from the shame of promiscuity. I want you to know that I see you. And I know that God longs to heal your heart so that you can live in the goodness of what He has for you. *God heals the hurts of the past to free you up for your purpose in the present.*

Prayer Prompt

God, You are fully aware of all that I have lived through. I open my heart to receive the healing You desire so that I'm able to live free.

PLEASING PAM

Pam, a divorced single mom, works as a salesperson at a local department store. At work she's known as a dedicated employee. In her neighborhood she's known as the one who's always there to lend a hand. At church she's the one who always says yes when she's asked to serve on a committee. In her family Pam is the one everyone depends on. She shows up to help when someone has a flood, a surgery, or needs a babysitter. She volunteers for all her daughter's activities at school and church. And while a lot of her activity is noble and serves others, there's a way in which her drive to stay busy, her addiction to pleasing others, hasn't served *Pam* well.

The view behind the closed doors of Pam's home tells the real story. Pam doesn't sleep well and depends on pills to rest at all. She doesn't like spending time alone because she's not comfortable with stillness or silence. If she was honest, she's not comfortable with herself. So, she fills the space by serving others in ways that aren't always healthy. The most important thing to Pam is how others view her. Pam's sense of self depends on the opinions of others. And that desperate need keeps Pam bound.

Pam is a people pleaser.

Pam is an amped-up version of what a lot of us struggle with. If we're not yet living free in the way God intended, we care about what others think of us. What they think of our appearance. What they think of how we speak. What they think of what we own. *When we're still bound, we are bullied by the opinions of others.*

And the conflict, when it comes to all that God has for us, is that the voices of all those other people drown out God's gentle voice. When those voices are loud, we fail to hear the one who speaks to us daily and helps us discern how He wants us to live. When we're tuned in to the voices and opinions of others, we fail to hear His voice.

God created Pam to live in freedom, but her choices are keeping her bound.

 Prayer Prompt

Daddy, You know the ways I'm tempted to please others. Give me a heart that hungers to please only You.

UNSUPPORTED UNIQUE

The final woman I want you to meet is Unique. Unique is married to a man who doesn't *see* her. Sure, he sees a wife. He sees a sexual object. He sees the mother of his children. He sees a housekeeper. A chauffer. A secretary. A social planner. But beyond what Unique provides for *him*, her husband doesn't see the Unique that God created her to be.

He doesn't delight in the stories he's heard about Unique as a girl, when she developed a friendship with a lonely elderly woman in her community. He doesn't care that she spent a summer with Habitat for Humanity, building houses for the less fortunate. He doesn't remember that she sold more Girl Scout cookies than any scout in the state. He doesn't celebrate her near-perfect SAT score, or her courage for doing standup as a college freshman, or her kindness in finding housing for a homeless woman she met on a mission trip. Unique's husband is not a bad guy, but he's simply unaware of Unique's *unique* design.

When Unique met her husband, she dropped out of college so that she could support him while he started his auto part supply business. Once his business was thriving, she suggested returning to school to get her degree. Unfortunately, he always dissuaded her, saying that he needed her at the front desk.

Unique—and the unique potential inside her—is unseen.

I suspect your story is different from Unique's, but maybe you can still relate. Maybe your parents had big dreams for your brothers but expected little from you. Maybe you had a big dream as a girl—to be a missionary, or a dancer, or an entrepreneur—and you were told to pursue something more sensible. Or maybe you've recently caught a glimpse of another woman doing something you know you'd love to do: direct a ministry, or work as an architect, or be a nurse. But when you mention it to someone you trust, your dream is met with silence or a discouraging word. You lack friends, family, or a trusted person who notices your unique gifts and passions and pushes you in that divine direction.

Prayer Prompt

Jesus, You are the one I need to see, hear, and support me most. You are more than enough for me.

Thankfully, others don't have the final say on our destiny. The One who took His time to design us is so clear about the path He has destined for us. God is the greatest guide we need to become the woman He desires us to be. If we sit around waiting on the approval of others to become who we were created to be, we may never discover this version of ourselves. But as we begin to look toward the One who knows us most intimately, the One who created us, He will help us to discover and embrace the unique purpose and permission He has granted to us.

JESUS' UNDERSTANDING OF WHO HE WAS

Did you recognize any of your own story in these women's stories? Ask God to open your eyes. If you're ever to get free, or go further in the freedom you already possess, it's critical to notice the things that are slowing you down. While it may not be in every area, there is an area in which God is moving you forward. Slow down. Hear the Lord. Ask Him to show you what your next season of freedom is supposed to look like.

And if you want to see what it looks like to live a life of permission, look at Jesus. In every moment He owned who He was and why He was created. He never released His firm grip on His identity as God's beloved Son.

At the beginning of Jesus' ministry, people He'd grown up with mocked Him by asking, "Isn't this Joseph's son?" (Luke 4:22). You can almost hear them asking, "Who's your daddy?" But Jesus knew exactly who He was:

- When these same people tried to toss Him off a cliff (Luke 4:29), furious that He claimed to be a prophet, Jesus was unconcerned. He didn't need the approval of others because He knew who He was.
- When religious leaders threw shade at Jesus for spending time with sinners (Luke 5:30), implying that He couldn't be holy, Jesus ignored them. He knew exactly who He was.
- When religious leaders interrogated Jesus, trying to trip Him up to prove He wasn't God's Son (Luke 11:53), Jesus wasn't moved by their badgering. He didn't need to prove Himself because He knew exactly who He was.
- When Jesus entered the temple to cast out those who were desecrating His Father's house (Luke 19:45), He was filled with passion for the sake of His Father's name. That's because Jesus knew exactly who He was.
- When Jesus was betrayed by His friend Judas (Luke 22:4), a betrayal that put Jesus in danger, He never questioned His identity. Jesus knew exactly who He was.

- And in His final hours, as a mob cried for Jesus' execution (Luke 23:23), He could have denied who He was. He could have saved His own life by pretending He wasn't God's Son. But Jesus was so very clear about His identity—as God's beloved Son—that He suffered and died for the sake of clinging to the *truth* of that identity!

Sis, when we read about Jesus, it can be tempting to think that the life of this ancient Middle Eastern man is nothing like our own lives. As we wrestle to live as the precise versions of ourselves that God intended us to be, we can forget that He faced the same identity challenges that we do.

The community where He grew up thought they knew who He was. But they didn't.

Those around Him couldn't see that He was God's beloved child.

People didn't understand why He spent time with those who had bad reputations.

Religious people rejected Him.

He was passionate about the holiness of His Father's house.

He was done wrong by a friend.

And, in the end, He was brutally beaten simply because He was who He knew that He was: *God's beloved.*

So when I challenge you to be precisely and fully who God created you to be, you can have the confidence that Jesus has walked this path ahead of you. Jesus knows what it's like when the world tells you that you're someone other than who you are. And He's modeled for us what it looks like to embrace exactly who God made us to be.

As you decide to anchor yourself in the truth of who God says you are, I want you to look specifically at Jesus in the third and fourth chapters of Matthew's gospel. As the third chapter concludes, we see Jesus being baptized by John. And a voice comes from heaven and says, "This is My beloved Son, in whom I am well pleased" (Matthew 3:17 NKJV). That is the voice of the Father, identifying Jesus as His own. And it's the same voice that calls *you* His own. This was prior to Jesus doing even one miracle or any amazing accomplishment on Earth. We can't miss this! Before we do anything, we are already considered beloved by God. His love for us isn't a response to what we do. Beloved, it's simply who we are. Loved. It's our godly identity.

Throughout Scripture we're reminded of our undeniable identity as God's daughters:

- **Jesus was God's child, and you are God's child.** "He predestined us to adoption as sons and daughters through Jesus Christ to Himself, according to the good pleasure of His will." (Ephesians 1:5 NASB)
- **Jesus reflected God's image, and you reflect God's image.** "So God created mankind in his own image, in the image of God he created them; male and female he created them." (Genesis 1:27)

- **Jesus was an heir of the Father, and you are an heir of the Father.** "Now if we are children, then we are heirs—heirs of God and co-heirs with Christ, if indeed we share in his sufferings in order that we may also share in his glory." (Romans 8:17)
- **Jesus was God's masterpiece, and you are God's masterpiece.** "For we are God's masterpiece." (Ephesians 2:10 NLT)
- **Jesus was loved, and you are loved.** "For I am convinced that neither death nor life, neither angels nor demons, neither the present nor the future, nor any powers, neither height nor depth, nor anything else in all creation, will be able to separate us from the love of God that is in Christ Jesus our Lord." (Romans 8:38–39)
- **Jesus reflected the Father, and you are being re-created to reflect the Father.** "You were taught . . . to be made new in the attitude of your minds; and to put on the new self, created to be like God in true righteousness and holiness." (Ephesians 4:22–24)
- **Jesus was spiritually blessed by God, and you are spiritually blessed by God.** "Praise be to the God and Father of our Lord Jesus Christ, who has blessed us in the heavenly realms with every spiritual blessing in Christ." (Ephesians 1:3)

Sis, I don't want you to read these scriptures just once! I want you to mark this page and allow these words to become your daily affirmation. As you commit to believing what God says about who you are, let these words become your new daily self-talk.

Immediately after His baptism, Jesus was led by the Spirit into the wilderness. For forty days and nights He fasted. And when that time was over, He was just as hungry as you'd be if you hadn't eaten for forty days. And this was the moment, when Jesus was so physically weak, that He was tested and tempted by the devil.

While the name "Beloved" was still echoing in Jesus' ears, after forty days and nights without food, the devil's entire strategy of attack was to question His identity. Consider the Scriptures below (italics are mine):

- "*If* you are the Son of God, tell these stones to become bread" (Matthew 4:3). You can almost hear the voices of those neighbors who didn't believe He was God's Son.
- "*If* You are the Son of God, throw Yourself down; for it is written: 'He will give his angels orders concerning you,' and 'On their hands they will lift you up, so that you do not strike your foot against a stone'" (Matthew 4:6 NASB). You can almost hear the voices of those religious leaders who challenged Jesus' identity.
- "All these [kingdoms] I will give You, *if* You fall down and worship me" (Matthew 4:9 NASB). You can almost hear those voices taunting Jesus when He was on the cross, tempting Him to forsake His Father and save

Himself. It's really a clever strategy, and it's exactly the one the enemy uses on us today!

And in every single instance, Jesus confirmed His identity as God's beloved Son by responding with the truth of God's Word: "It is written . . ."

Here's a challenge I want you to try out.

- If someone says, "You're not really God's daughter. If you were, you would have all the money and resources you needed," then you can say, "It is written, 'My God will meet all your needs according to the riches of his glory in Christ Jesus'" (Philippians 4:19).
- If someone says, "You're not really God's daughter. If you were then you wouldn't be in this situation," then you can say, "Jesus answered, 'It is said: "Do not put the Lord your God to the test"'" (Luke 4:12).
- If someone says, "I'll give you whatever you want if you just worship me," then you can say, "It is written: 'Do not worship any other god, for the LORD, whose name is Jealous, is a jealous God'" (Exodus 34:14).

Just as Jesus answered the lies of the enemy with what was written in God's Word, so can we.

Citing God's Word, Jesus chose to trust God.

Standing on Scripture, He refused to test God.

Reciting Scripture, He vowed to worship only His Father.

This is exactly what it looks like to live a life of permission!

Jesus knew exactly who He was: the Beloved Son. And He knew exactly what He was made for: to know and glorify His Father. He was so secure in that identity, even in His physically weakened state, that He never once wavered from the reality of who God made Him to be.

This is how we can live a life of permission too. We refuse to allow others to define us. We refuse to allow others to determine our behavior. We refuse to allow others to tempt us. And because we're so securely grounded in our identity in Christ, the enemy will be forced to flee.

Even beyond this iconic moment we see of Jesus in the wilderness, He didn't get a break from temptation. Haters accused Him of being a glutton. They slandered Him by calling Him a friend of sinners. They disrespected Him when He hung on the cross. And yet no opinion of man ever caused Jesus to waver from His clear certainty about His identity. Because He knew He was God's beloved, people's lack of understanding of who He was, their doubts, didn't bother Him. He was unwilling to release the permission He'd received from His Father. He was solid and firmly anchored.

Sis, when you are living in the fullness of who you were created to be, people *will* have something to say about you. But the full truth is, even if you don't choose to, they will still have something to say. So you may as well choose freedom! Again and again God will strengthen you and equip you to stand in the truth of who you really are. And I want you to do it in every room you walk into. I want you to exude, "I don't have anything to prove. I know who I am."

PERMISSION IS NOT WHAT YOU DO

I don't want you to confuse your unique purpose, which has been given by God, with permission. They're related, but they're not the same. *Permission is about who you are, not what you do.* However, it's the underpinning that causes you to do the thing you've been created for.

As we seek God for our purpose in life, it can be tempting to put the cart before the horse. We want to know what to do before we ever know who we are. Do you see the difference? We believe the lie that what we do is what makes us significant. When in reality we are already loved by God, which gives us significance and value and wholeness. Permission is about owning the essence of who God created you to be from the very beginning. Simply put: if you didn't do a thing, if you stayed home and never got out of bed, God would still count you as a masterpiece.

This said, the reality is that God does have work for you to do! And I hope you hear that as good news. Paul reminded first-century Jesus followers that "we are God's handiwork, created in Christ Jesus to do good works, which God prepared in advance for us to do" (Ephesians 2:10). When God created you to be uniquely you, He imagined the good works you would do! But your value to God does not depend on you doing anything *for* God. You are already loved, and the good works you do are simply a natural *response* to that love.

How does that hit you? Is that hard for your heart to receive? *Surely God wouldn't look at me lying in bed and think*

I'm a masterpiece . . . If you find yourself resisting—which, of course, I understand—I want you to pause and notice that. Carve out some time to spend with God and look at your resistance. Don't take my word for it either. *Ask* God: "If I have nothing and I can't do anything for you, do you still love me? Am I still your beloved?" Then *listen.* Let God speak His truth to your heart.

This is a truth that can transform your life!

=== **Embrace Permission Exercise** ===

1. When you look at the lives of these five women, where do you see glimpses of your own life? Where do you hear echoes of your own heart?
2. In what ways, today, does your comfort interfere with your true identity?
3. In what ways, today, does fear interfere with your freedom?
4. In what ways, today, do the hurts from your past still have an enduring impact in your life?
5. In what ways, today, are you being bullied by your concern with the opinions of others?
6. In what ways, today, are you lacking support to be who you really are?

=== **Prayer** ===

Let's pray together.

Daddy, although the enemy comes to steal, kill, and destroy, I believe that Your Son came so that I could have life, and life abundantly! I ask, in Jesus' name, for You to come for the comfort, the fear, the trauma, the people-pleasing, and the lack of support that attempt to stifle me from owning the true essence of who You made me to be. Amen.

FOUR

PERMISSION TO RELEASE OLD WAYS OF LIVING

Do not conform to the pattern of this world, but
be transformed by the renewing of your mind.

ROMANS 12:2

I DON'T THINK WE EVER PURPOSE TO LIVE IN A FAKE, PRE-
tend, or counterfeit way. But I do think that our lives have
been shaped by our early experiences and daily choices. The
hurts we've endured shape us. The opinions we give ear to
guide the way we choose to live. But when you look at the life
of Courtney, you just see *Courtney*. When you pass Frieda at
the mall, you just see *Frieda*. When you sit beside Tammy at
a sporting event, she's just *Tammy*. There's no flashing neon
sign over them announcing Comfortable Courtney! Fearful
Frieda! Traumatized Tammy! Pleasing Pam! Unsupported
Unique!

The women we know as our sisters and friends are just
themselves, right?

Yes and no.

Yes, they're precious individuals, created by God, who've
endured the same kinds of bumps and bruises we all have
along their journey. But they may not be the most authentic
versions of themselves. So many of the ways that they protect
themselves from being hurt again, or adjust who they are to
please others, mean that they're not yet living in the fullness
of what God has for them. And the same is true for our lives.

And in the absence of those helpful neon signs, some
of us are left wondering whether the life we see before us is

counterfeit or authentic—many times because it's the only life we've ever known. There's no value in judging other women for the ways they are or aren't being authentic, but there is *great value* in weighing whether we ourselves are living authentically.

If we're hungry to become the truest version of ourselves, we're going to have to be willing to open our lives up for inspection. The good news is that we don't have to invite the whole neighborhood. This is between you and God. And as I share the signs of a counterfeit life, I welcome you to notice which ones might identify you, in some small or large way. And as we continue this journey, you'll have the opportunity to address these. But for the moment, your job is simply to notice.

FIVE SIGNS OF COUNTERFEIT LIVING

1. The woman living a counterfeit life fails to prioritize a vibrant, personal relationship with God.

"But seek first his kingdom and his righteousness, and all these things will be given to you as well" (Matthew 6:33).

Let's be honest: it's easier to let a relationship slide—with a friend, a relative, a colleague, a neighbor—than to nurture, water, feed, and grow it. And what's true of our relationships with people is true of our relationship with God. What's most convenient, what's *easiest*, is to put a relationship on standard mode. And then we rationalize to convince ourselves that it's all good.

I went to church on Sunday, so I'm good.

I read a Bible verse on a card my grandma sent me, so I'm good.

I prayed before dinner, so I'm good.

I hollered God's name when I hit my toe, so I'm good.

I've known God for decades, so . . . I'm good.

Yeah, I know it sounds corny. But when we're in a season where we've let our relationship with God slide, our minds do these mental gymnastics to justify our choices. And the withdrawal might actually sneak up on us. Maybe we begin to opt for an extra hour of sleep rather than getting up to spend time with God. Or we blame our retreat from relationship with Him on having a hectic schedule. We come up with all kinds of excuses to justify failing to make God a priority.

And on the outside we might be looking good. People might think well of us because we show up for everyone else. We're busy with good things. But we don't give the time and space to focus on what's important to God: relationship.

When Unique got to college, she saw her roommate living differently because she knew Christ. As a result of this friendship and the contagious witness of her friend, Unique came to know Christ for herself. And she was absolutely on fire for God. When she dropped out of college to support her husband's business, she no longer found time to spend with friends like her roommate who encouraged her walk with the

Lord. Long hours at work crowded out the time she'd previously committed to going to church and spending personal time with God.

Unique never intentionally abandoned God. But she allowed other things to interfere with the ways she encountered Him. Although she never intended to deceive anyone, Unique was living a counterfeit life because it wasn't the real thing God intended for her. Without genuine, consistent connection with the Lord, we are also disconnected from the greatest source of truth and authenticity. We keep ourselves outside of the Good Shepherd's leading. Our lives were designed to accomplish His will, but it's impossible to do this without consistent and meaningful connection with Him.

2. The woman living a counterfeit life clings to the "extras" that fail to give her worth.

"Are not two sparrows sold for a penny? Yet not one of them will fall to the ground outside your Father's care. And even the very hairs of your head are all numbered. So don't be afraid; you are worth more than many sparrows" (Matthew 10:29–31).

The woman living a counterfeit life might not even consciously realize that she's trusting in extra things, but they drive her. And she believes that if she achieves them, she'll finally be worthy.

When I get married, I'll be worthy.

When I get the degree after my name, I'll be worthy.

When I get the house, I'll be worthy.

When I lose the weight, I'll be worthy.

When I get one hundred thousand followers, I'll be worthy.

When I become a mom, I'll be worthy.

Well, the devil is a liar. And this is one of his favorite deceptions. He convinces us that our value can somehow be achieved if we do this and don't do that, get this, and lose that. And so we rush, strive, and live discontentedly, but in the end we're still empty. When we pin our worth to any person, goal, or achievement, we will never know our true value that is found only in God.

Remember Comfortable Courtney? She's an attractive attorney with the house, the Benz, the hubby, the kids, the dog, and the designer bag. She looks like she has it all together. She appears to be living her best life. But the problem is that those exterior things are covering up what's inside her. On the inside, Courtney has no idea that she's God's beloved. She doesn't know that her worth has absolutely nothing to do with the six-figure income. Despite all the external frills, Courtney isn't secure in her value as someone designed and created by God. And so she's anchored her worth to the things she has. And she's afraid to release any of them because she's simply not convinced that she is undeniably worthy and loved by God. The life she's living is counterfeit—it's not the life God intended for her to live.

3. The woman living a counterfeit life strives to please people rather than receiving the truth of who she is from God.

"Do not conform to the pattern of this world, but be transformed by the renewing of your mind" (Romans 12:2).

This woman doesn't receive her identity from God. She isn't in fellowship with those who are able to affirm who she *really* is in God, so she looks for validation from others. And because she's not spending time with God, she hasn't given Him room—and permission—to transform her mind and her life!

She might be stuck in a harmful relationship because she needs affirmation. She might even be holding on so tightly to her man, because she wants a husband, that she'll ultimately delay God's good plan for her because what she wants gets in the way. I sometimes say this woman thinks of herself as Jesus Junior. She thinks *she's* sovereign.

She might be stubbornly bent on pursuing the path her family expects of her.

She might be driving herself into the ground in the name of serving others.

But because her ear isn't turned toward God's voice, she cannot be set free. She is much more willing to believe what the world says about her than what God says about her. She's so busy trying to please others that she loses sight of trying to see things the way God does—by allowing Him to transform her mind. And she neglects to choose His way because she is trying to please others rather than recognizing that God's way is best.

She fears that if she's not pleasing others she will be abandoned. And, as a result, she *never* feels affirmed as the unique woman God made her to be. Not only does this woman ignore and reject the truth of who God made her to be, she spends time with those who also fail to affirm the truth of who she is.

Pam, the people pleaser, is busy doing all sorts of good things for others. But as a pleaser, she seeks validation from others rather than from God. If she gets enough likes on a social media post, she feels good. If there aren't enough likes, she feels as though she is worth *less*. And while Pam isn't that girl who seeks out affection in clubs with strange men, she is in a relationship in which she compromises her moral standards to hold on to a man she hopes will validate her.

Yet the appreciation of others, bringing snacks to every one of her daughter's games, the comments on Instagram, the attention of the boyfriend who's using her—it's never enough to satisfy Pam. Without the affirmation of her truest identity, which only God can provide, she continues to seek it from those who can never satisfy.

 Prayer Prompt

Father, show me the area of my life in which I care more about the opinions of others than I do about Your opinion of me.

PERMISSION TO LIVE FREE

4. The woman living a counterfeit life refuses to face the truth.

"Then you will know the truth, and the truth will set you free" (John 8:32).

In situation after situation this woman will choose to believe a lie—either subtle or outright—rather than doing the hard work of looking at what's true about herself, true about others, and true about God. She is content believing that her identity lies in what she has, what she does, and what others think of her. And, as a result, she never enters into the freedom that comes from embracing the truth of her identity in Christ.

This woman living a counterfeit life also ignores the hurts of her past.

When memories of past abuse bubble to the surface, she self-soothes by binge-watching Netflix and taking sleeping pills.

When she's forced to be with a person who bullied her in the past, she puts on a façade and smiles her way through the encounter.

When she's triggered and reminded of her father's abandonment, she acts as if she's fine with it.

When a faithful friend or caring relative brings up the hurt in her past, she refuses to discuss it.

I see the impact of emotional trauma in the lives of women who won't face the hurts of the past. And sadly, this woman can be very walled off. Anxious. Insecure. Sometimes she suffers from depression.

70

Hear me: This isn't an evil woman; this is a *hurting* woman. She learned defenses to avoid feeling pain, and those defenses feel more reliable than taking the risk of trusting God with her tender places. And so she remains stuck in counterfeit living.

Traumatized Tammy is this hurting woman. She's believed the enemy's lie that if she avoids looking at what happened to her, if she refuses to face the pain, it won't affect her. She's not yet realized that the opposite is actually more true! She doesn't know that the way to healing is actually to face the pain head on. Until Tammy gathers her courage to bring her hurts before the Lord, and ideally a good therapist, she will continue to suffer.

5. The woman living a counterfeit life settles for "good enough."

"The thief comes only to steal and kill and destroy; I have come that they may have life, and have it to the full" (John 10:10).

The enemy of great is good. And when we settle for good enough, we may be refusing God's *greatest* for us. Jesus didn't come for us to have good enough. He came for us to have life in abundance. He wants to give us extravagant life, and we refuse it when we settle for good enough.

The woman who lives in isolation when she has so much to offer the sphere of influence God has called her to has settled for good enough.

The woman who has poured her heart into her job but has failed to pursue meaningful relationships outside of work, with God and with godly women, has settled for good enough.

The woman who's garnered all the things—the job, the family, the home, the vacations—but has never asked God how she can be a builder of God's kingdom has settled for good enough.

And because she's content with good enough, it's as if she's wearing blinders, unable to see what is better. She can't see the calling, the career, the relationships, the purpose that are God's best for her because she's settled.

Frieda, who is bound by fear, is afraid that her appearance isn't good enough, her home isn't good enough, her education isn't good enough, her personality isn't good enough. And as a result—ironically—she has settled for good enough! And although technically her job and home and family are good enough, Frieda's fear has kept her from pursuing God's *best* for her. She has been called according to God's good purpose, but rather than gather her courage to pursue the powerful prophetic ministry for which God has gifted her, she has resigned herself to good enough.

A PEEK AT MY FREEDOM

You know I had issues with my hair. And as a result, I became a specialist in covering up one of my most vulnerable areas. After being teased when I was younger, I internally vowed that I would never give anybody else another opportunity to have an opinion about my hair. I could still hear the voices of my brother, cousins, and even friends at school making fun of me. I remembered being emotionally scarred by their looks and the whispered remarks. I wore hair extensions for as long as I can remember. Extensions became a part of my new identity that I embraced so fully that when my mom would suggest my wearing my natural hair, I would remark, "Yeah Mom, that's just not me!"

In a season when I was stepping more fully into permission, I sat in front of my hairdresser, Flo, and told her I was ready for the big-chop haircut. For years I'd worn this cute, curly, protective style. Full curls framed my face and fell to just above my shoulders. And I'd gotten comfortable there.

But as I was stepping into the new, I felt it was imperative to fully embrace all it had to offer. I removed the curly extensions, uncovered my natural head of hair, and asked Flo to cut it all off.

As she began cutting away years of insecurity and pain, I panicked. "Hold on. Stop! Wait . . ."

I was afraid. I was actually shaking. I began to cry! I didn't know how it would look.

Flo helped me settle back down and kept cutting. When she finished, I looked in the mirror to see the hair on the sides of my head completely shaved off, and just a few inches of my natural curls on top!

As she spun me around to fully take in this look from all angles, I noticed that my fear dissipated. And what I felt was something new. It was freedom!

As God calls you into the new, you might feel scared and shaky. You might even protest: "Hold on. Stop! Wait . . ."

But as you gather the courage to step through that door, to move into the new thing that God has for you, you just might experience a freedom you've never felt before. What freedom will look like in your life, when you stop pretending and stop covering up, will likely be unique to you.

One woman who'd been a stay-at-home mom for fifteen years chose to step back into her work clothes and into the new career she'd been waiting to launch.

Another woman who'd been single for forty-three years was at last walking down the aisle in a lacy white gown.

Another woman took the risk of taking off the business suit she wore as a litigator and slipping into her apron to open that bakery she always dreamed of!

It's no coincidence that all these life changes require a new garment. Just like my haircut, the suit and the gown and the apron all signaled a new season. Ask God to show you the signs—spiritually and maybe even physically—that He's inviting you into a new season of permission.

Whether it's a big chop or a different kind of shift, God is welcoming you to *stop pretending*. Do you see how dangerous living in falsehood can be? When we pretend, when we cover up, we reject who God created us to be. There were very few seasons when I wore my hair natural, and it was never for long because I always felt something was wrong with my hair. I felt naked without my extensions. Even after my hair grew back and became healthy, I was still so damaged in this area.

Damaged hair.

Damaged girl.

So I covered up.

Once you become comfortable with covering up, conforming in other ways always seems to follow.

Prayer Prompt

Lord, open the eyes of my heart. Show me how I have conformed or pretended or covered up to appear other than who I am.

YOUR STORY

I've taken the time to share real-life scenarios from a variety of women, most importantly for you to know you are not alone in your fight to be free. My prayer is that as you recognized yourself in portions of these ladies' stories, it was a love tap from the Lord, for you to know He only exposes what He desires to grow, nurture, and ultimately heal.

The call is to progression, not perfection. All the growth you desire to see won't happen overnight. But with your next *yes*, giving the Father access to what He made loud in your heart through these personas, you ensure you will be heading toward God's best for you!

═══ **Embrace Permission Exercise** ═══

Spend some time with the five signs of counterfeit living. They will become the answers to your prayers for change, as you are now able to give language to what you have been experiencing. It will help you navigate forward in the direction of freedom!

Where in my life does this sign of counterfeit living show itself?

a. I fail to prioritize a vibrant personal relationship with God.

b. I cling to the extras that fail to give me worth.

c. I strive to please people rather than receiving the truth of who I am from God.

d. I refuse to face the truth.

e. I settle for "good enough."

═══════════════════════ **Prayer** ═══

Let's pray together.

Lord, ignite in my soul an unwavering commitment to be transformed into the likeness of Jesus and to become who You made me to be. I want nothing more. As You identify areas in my life that are counterfeit, please transform me through the renewing of my heart and mind. In Jesus' name, amen.

FIVE

PERMISSION TO LIVE LOVED

> Then God said, "Let us make human beings in our
> image, to be like us." . . . So God created human
> beings in his own image. In the image of God he
> created them; male and female he created them.

GENESIS 1:26–27 NLT

WHEN I WAS A FOUR-YEAR-OLD GIRL, TESTIFYING TO OTHERS about the power of God was normal—I was free. And I would guess that when you were a girl, you were free too.

Maybe you liked to wear mismatched socks. Or sneakers.

Maybe you stood up to the neighborhood bully, defending someone more vulnerable, without flinching.

Or you might have stood proudly on stage and sung like no one was watching. When absolutely *everyone* was watching.

Freedom has always been God's good plan for us! His design, when He created Adam and Eve, was that we would be naked and unashamed. It's the world that taught us to break off a fig leaf, to cover up and hide when we have a misstep or lose our way. It's the world that taught us to be concerned about what other people think when they see our bodies. When they hear our voices. When we take a risk. But God created us for freedom. For nakedness. For authenticity. For transparency. God meant for us to walk in the cool of the day with Him— talking and singing and shouting—without shame.

Sister, when I was a girl, I was free! I was so bold and unapologetic about the way God made me! I gave no thought to what people would think or the question "What if I don't do this right?" Failure wasn't an option, so I pursued all that I felt led by God to do. I lived in the freedom of my truth. I was secure in who God was, which made me secure in who I was. When we're young, when we're girls, we don't stop to ask where our security comes from.

Before I even understood what the permission journey was, I loved who I was! I was okay with being the only one who looked and acted like me. I was a passionate, genuine lover of Jesus. I think God was intentional about my initial encounters with Him happening during a time when I was fearless, affirmed, and encouraged to worship God from a fully surrendered place.

That girl, that freedom, that sure identity in God, is what owning your permission feels like.

OUR FREEDOM IS ROOTED IN LOVE

At the time, I couldn't have told you why I felt so free. Or why other children are also able to embrace freedom in a way that makes many adults jealous. But today I know where my freedom comes from. *My freedom, and your freedom, comes from being fully and completely loved by God.*

When we know that God delights in us, we don't have to worry about what others think of us.

When we're rooted in God's love for us, we're secure.

When we're convinced that a loving God made us on purpose, exactly the way that we are, we can live in freedom.

Have you ever observed a woman who knows in her deep places that she is loved by God? Her face is free of anxiety.

She's joyful. She's confident. She's able to be fully present to others. She's radiant! When we rest in God's love for us, we're able to become the unique women God made us to be. *To live loved is to be fully free.*

WHAT ABOUT YOU?

How did life begin for you? Were you that fierce, fearless girl who shouted and sang and lived in a world of her own?

As you look back at your earliest days, ask God to give you the vision to see with fresh eyes the unique person He made you to be. What gave you joy? What occupied you for hours? What were your passions?

Maybe you'll remember a word that was spoken over you in your earliest days. Maybe a person of influence noticed your ability to lead, to love, or to create. Maybe when you look at the girl you were, you'll see someone who was bold, fearless, and full of hope. And I don't want you to miss this if your boldness or freedom didn't look the same as everyone else's. Boldness and freedom show up differently in each life. Maybe you weren't outspoken, but you were internally sure. Maybe you didn't approach every newcomer, but you were confident to be just who you were without compromise! I'm talking about inner strength and boldness to not sell out on who you truly were and what you truly felt. I want you to remember that fearless girl.

A lot of us begin life so sure of ourselves. We were born

an authentic, raw, choice treasure, fashioned by the hand of God. The prophet Isaiah announced, "Yet you, LORD, are our Father. We are the clay, you are the potter; we are all the work of your hand" (Isaiah 64:8). It's so amazing that when we were young, most of us were so daring. We learned that our voice made noise, and we made the loudest noise we could. We found out that walking wasn't as hard as we thought, so we dared to start running! We sang without regard for who was listening. We loved in a way that was pure and genuine. We believed in others with such faith that it caused others to believe in themselves.

Can you remember the things you wore as a child? The purple-and-yellow polka-dot dress with the red rain boots that you frequently wore because it was your favorite outfit and it made you happy. Or what about the Teenage Mutant Ninja Turtles shirt with the red-and-white striped shorts? Maybe you were able to put this combination together only because you were at home with your dad and knew he loved it when you exerted your independence to choose.

Before we learn to be concerned with other people's opinion of us, we are free. We are not devoid of the innate desire to make our parental figures proud, but our whole life is not dictated by what someone else is thinking. And while you may not remember it, there was a precious time in your life when you did not care one bit about what others thought of you— but not in an unhealthy or limiting way.

Wouldn't it be great if we could live like that forever?

For many of us, the earliest years of our lives were the ones when we weren't yet wounded by the inevitable bumps and bruises of life. We trusted that our caregivers were always going to be with us and for us. We weren't yet aware of obstacles we or our loved ones would face: addiction, illness, abandonment, divorce, abuse, poverty, or unemployment. Before we were ever emotionally hurt by others, we were free from internal wounds. We endured hurts, but we weren't being *bossed around* by the hurts we'd suffered.

Wouldn't it be great if we could live like that forever?

As you grew, though, you became aware that you were separate from your caregivers. As you began to experience your first episodes with emotional hurt, it turned your eyes outward. And—just like everyone else—you began looking to the world for affirmation. But this is always a losing game. *The world will never give us unconditional love.* The world will scream that we're less than we really are. It will convince us to act as if we're more than we really are. And it will even woo us into playing charades as we imitate who we want to be. But the world will never give us permission to be the person that God created us to be.

 Prayer Prompt

Lord, show me the ways I lived in my freedom as a girl, and open my eyes to the ways in which I became bound.

THE LOVE WE WERE MADE FOR

Although the world won't give us the love we were made for, or permission to be fully who we are, some of us have experienced little tastes of the love that is special.

Has there been anyone in your life who has loved you unconditionally? Maybe a grandmother got a twinkle in her eye whenever she saw you, and you knew you were fully accepted. Maybe a grandfather taught you how to fish or to swing a bat, and you knew you were loved. Maybe an auntie took you shopping for clothes that really expressed who you were, and you felt seen. Maybe a counselor offered you a gentle, listening ear, and you knew you were heard. Or maybe a husband took the time to discover everything about you, and you finally felt known.

Many of us have had these encounters that made us feel loved. As human beings it's what we hunger for. But what we've learned is that although we can experience love from the important people in our lives, human love isn't *perfect* love. It can be really special, but ultimately there is only one love that never fails.

BELOVED

Recently I've been reading the book *You Are Beloved* by Bobby Schuller, the grandson of popular preacher Robert Schuller. Bobby says he was at the Crystal Cathedral when he came across video teachings of Catholic priest and author Henri Nouwen, who preached in the famous sanctuary. Calling it the most important sermon he's ever heard, Bobby shares that Nouwen's words were the clearest picture of grace he's ever heard: "You're not what you do. You're not what you have. You're not what people say about you. You are the beloved of God."[1]

Although my life experience is radically different from that of either Bobby Schuller or Henri Nouwen, who was reared in the Netherlands, those words also powerfully impacted me because they speak to that concern we have with the opinions of others. They name what is so very true about the way the world identifies us. Daily we're told that our value lies in what we do—the job we have, the role we play, the relationships that define us. The world shouts that our worth is contingent on what we have—the car, the house, the wardrobe, the bank account. And the constant chatter in our heads insists that what matters most is what other people think and say about us.

It's exhausting, right? It's too much.

But Nouwen, and then Schuller, insist that none of those things define us. What identifies who we truly are is the fact that we belong to God and are loved by Him. That's it! It doesn't matter what we do, what we have, or what other people say. The only thing that matters is that you and I are the beloved of God.

I want you to say it aloud. Now. Wherever you are:

I am the beloved of God.

I want you to say it before you drift off to sleep tonight. I want you to say it the moment you wake up in the morning. I want you to say it when you look in the mirror and when you take a selfie. I want you to say it out loud until it is the constant song of the Lord over your life that remains on repeat.

I am the beloved of God.

Can you even begin to imagine a life in which what you do, what you have, and what people say about you didn't define you? Instead your identity rests completely on the foundational reality that you are the beloved of God. It's just as mind-blowing as you think it might be.

We're used to settling. We settle for "mom." We settle for "stockbroker." We settle for "artist." We settle for "pastor." And there's nothing inherently wrong with those titles. But they are not enough to build our lives on. They're transient. They can be taken from us. And whenever the identifier we've built our life on evaporates, we find ourselves lost and searching. A lot of us aren't aware of how much weight we put on what people think of us. And that's a danger. When we craft a life that's built on the opinions of others, we've created an unreliable identity.

You and I were created for so much more. We were created to be the *beloved* of God. That is the inherent essence of who we are. It's the anchor that grounds us in what is most true. And it was established before we took our first breath. It was a done deal. The apostle Paul reminded believers in Ephesus, "Even before he made the world, God loved us and chose us in Christ to be holy and without fault in his eyes"

(Ephesians 1:4 NLT). We didn't have to earn it. We didn't have to submit a resume of accomplishments. The identity of "beloved" was simply bestowed on us because *we belong to God.* You and I belong to God.

If you're like a lot of women I meet, you may recognize the magnitude of this life-changing truth but still notice a little resistance inside. You might quietly say to yourself, "It's too good to be true." Or, "It might be true for others, but not for me."

It is absolutely true about you as well.

God found you so worthy that He sent Jesus to die for you. Paul explained, "But God demonstrates his own love for us in this: While we were still sinners, Christ died for us" (Romans 5:8). He didn't send Jesus once you showered, put on your makeup, put on your cutest outfit, did your hair, and put on your favorite jewelry. He loved you so much that He died for you when you were at your worst, embracing a life of sin. He gave His best. For you.

We hear this in church, and sometimes we don't really receive it. But this reality of the gospel reminds me how very loved I am by God. And when I have those moments when I feel like I need to strive—for acceptance, for approval—the words of Paul ground me in what is most true about who I am.

What is happening inside you as you consider the reality of God's genuine love for you before you ever clean up your act?

Notice your reactions.

Notice the way it heals your heart.

Most of all, notice what would be different in your life if you received this transforming truth in your deepest places.

This reality, that you are God's beloved and He loved you before the creation of the world, is what is *most true about you*. And His love can be the anchor of your life.

In Paul's letter to the church in Galatia, he asked, "Am I now trying to win the approval of human beings, or of God? Or am I trying to please people? If I were still trying to please people, I would not be a servant of Christ" (Galatians 1:10). Paul's choice in the first century is the same choice we face today. We will either anchor our identity in the sure foundation that is our belovedness in God, or we will turn our eyes toward the opinion of men and women, getting yanked along on that roller-coaster ride.

HOLD ON TO THE TRUTH

The key to not being dragged up and down on the roller coaster of human opinion is to anchor your security in who God says you are. When you are reading your Bible and come across scriptures that confirm your truest identity, I encourage you to highlight them. Underline them. Scribble stars and exclamation points beside them! You can start with these . . .

- **You are God's daughter.** See what great love the Father has lavished on us, that we should be called children of God! And that is what we are! (1 John 3:1)
- **God loves you and is with you.** Since you are precious and honored in my sight, and because I love you, I will

give people in exchange for you. . . . Do not be afraid, for I am with you. (Isaiah 43:4–5)

- **You are God's masterpiece.** For we are God's masterpiece. (Ephesians 2:10 NLT)
- **You are loved by Jesus.** As the Father has loved me, so I have loved you. Now remain in my love. (John 15:9)
- **God's truth sets you free.** To the Jews who had believed him, Jesus said, "If you hold to my teaching, you are really my disciples. Then you will know the truth, and the truth will set you free." (John 8:31–32)

I can't stress enough how important it is to cling to the truth of who God says you are. So after you highlight your Bible, write one of these on an index card and tape it to your bathroom mirror. Speak it aloud every morning. Commit it to memory and speak it to someone you love. You defeat the lies of the enemy by announcing what is most true!

 Prayer Prompt

Daddy, when I'm tempted to believe a lie about who You made me to be, bring Your transforming truth to my mind.

HOW GOD MADE YOU

Sometimes I wonder how our lives would be different if we could return to the boldness and sureness of our youth. If we could live with a carefree audacity that requires us to accept our quirkiness, love ourselves, and embrace the things about us that others may mock or have an opinion about. Do you think that's possible?

I want to invite you to explore the possibility that the God who loves you designed you—as you are—*on purpose.* And I'm welcoming you as someone who's also on this permission journey every day. For a long time I beat myself up because I talk fast, love hard, cry easily, and I have fine hair that doesn't grow as rapidly as the hair of some other women. But as God worked inside me, I came to recognize that all these differences are what make me uniquely me. If God wanted any one of my emotional, physical, or personality traits to be different, He could have changed anything easily.

Over time, God has freed me from the pressure of wanting to be different. Instead, I began to embrace my difference! God's challenge to me, for as long as I can remember, has been to live my God-given truth and not embrace the lies of the world! I believe this challenge—to embrace the way God made each one of us—is His universal call to all His children. He has a desire for each of us to be genuine and authentic to the way He originally created us. For when the Father was done designing you and me, He saw masterpieces!

In this moment, I am asking God to ignite your holy imagination. In Psalm 139, the writer announced, "For you created my inmost being; you knit me together in my mother's womb" (v. 13). Imagine the God who loves you knitting you together in *your* mother's womb. And because God loves you,

God is carefully sculpting you *exactly as you are*. The kink of your hair. The curve of your hip. The height of your lip. The way you're drawn toward people. Or the fact you need time alone to recharge. The excitement you feel when _____. Or the way you get fired up about _____. Your Creator designed you exactly as you are and He loves every part of you. In fact, there's nothing you could do to cause God to love you any less. *Nothing.*

For many of us, this unearned favor is hard to wrap our minds around. Because we haven't experienced being loved unconditionally, exactly as we are, there's a part of us that finds it hard to believe. And if we can't believe it, we can't receive it.

The place where we discover what true love looks like is in Scripture. In his letter to a local church filled with people who were probably a lot like us, Paul let us glimpse the perfect love of God: "Love is patient, love is kind. It does not envy, it does not boast, it is not proud. It does not dishonor others, it is not self-seeking, it is not easily angered, it keeps no record of wrongs. Love does not delight in evil but rejoices with the truth. It always protects, always trusts, always hopes, always perseveres" (1 Corinthians 13:4–7).

That's how God loves us! His love is patient and kind. Not envious or boastful or proud. It doesn't diss people. It's not self-seeking. God's not angry or keeping score. God's love delights in the truth. God's love protects, trusts, hopes, and hangs in there.

But here's the thing. Those holy words—that are true—can

sometimes feel like *just words*. And as humans, we need to see love put into action. So, while I'm encouraging you to live loved, I want you to see what it looks like to live with this posture toward *yourself*. Here's what it looks like, on the ground, to live loved:

I am patient with myself.
I am kind toward myself.
I'm not envious of others.
I have no need to boast.
I'm not proud.
I don't dishonor myself.
I don't have to seek my own gain.
I'm not angry with myself.
I'm not keeping track of everything I do wrong.
I don't take pleasure in evil, but I rejoice in what's good.
I protect myself.
I trust myself.
I have hope.
I persevere.

That, Queen, is what it looks like to live loved! That's what it looks like when you accept that you are God's beloved and live in that reality. As God's love for you seeps into your deep places, you begin to have the same posture toward yourself that God already has toward you. And the Bible's words about God's love for you *come to life* as you live in the love God has for you. As you practice it. As you embrace it.

To live in God's love is to be fully free. I am convinced that from the beginning, God intended you to *be* free and to *stay* free. And that's the invitation of permission. Yes, if you choose to, you'll be free to wear polka dots and stripes and sparkles and glitter, without a care in the world for others' opinions. But you're also invited to rediscover the girl in you who knows herself to be completely loved by God. This girl is totally free. Free to sing. Free to dance. Free to draw. Free to keep silent. Free to serve. Free to give. Free to love. Free to excel. Free to forgive. Free to thrive. Free to try. *God's love for you sets you free.*

As I exhort you to live loved, I want to echo a prayer that Paul and Timothy prayed for some of Jesus' earliest followers in a city called Philippi: "And this is my prayer: that your love may abound more and more in knowledge and depth of insight, so that you may be able to discern what is best and may be pure and blameless for the day of Christ" (Philippians 1:9–10).

I pray that God, who loves you beyond all measure and who has already given you permission, will give you more insight into the abounding and unconditional love He has for you.

LIVE ROOTED IN LOVE

On the permission journey we can choose to live loved. So as you make this daily choice, I want to offer you some fuel, an arsenal of love scriptures. As you feast on these truths, allow them to feed and nourish your heart each day. Try to commit some to memory!

Since you are precious and honored in my sight, and because I love you, I will give people in exchange for you, nations in exchange for your life. (Isaiah 43:4)

Do everything in love. (1 Corinthians 16:14)

I pray that out of his glorious riches he may strengthen you with power through his Spirit in your inner being, so that Christ may dwell in your hearts through faith. And I pray that you, being rooted and established in love, may have power, together with all the Lord's holy people, to grasp how wide and long and high and deep is the love of Christ. (Ephesians 3:16–18)

May the Lord direct your hearts into God's love and Christ's perseverance. (2 Thessalonians 3:5)

And over all these virtues put on love, which binds them all together in perfect unity. (Colossians 3:14)

And so we know and rely on the love God has for us. God is love. Whoever lives in love lives in God, and God in them. (1 John 4:16)

Let the morning bring me word of your unfailing love, for I have put my trust in you. (Psalm 143:8)

We love because he first loved us. (1 John 4:19)

Above all, love each other deeply, because love covers over a multitude of sins. (1 Peter 4:8)

My command is this: Love each other as I have loved you. (John 15:12)

No one has ever seen God; but if we love one another, God lives in us and his love is made complete in us. (1 John 4:12)

Place me like a seal over your heart, like a seal on your arm; for love is as strong as death, its jealousy unyielding as the grave. It burns like blazing fire, like a mighty flame. (Song of Songs 8:6)

However, as it is written: "What no eye has seen, what no ear has heard, and what no human mind has conceived"— the things God has prepared for those who love him. (1 Corinthians 2:9)

=== **Embrace Permission Exercise** ===

1. Ask God to help you notice anything that might be holding you back from living in the abundant love He has for you.
2. Who is the person in your life who did, or does, offer you unconditional love?
3. On a scale of 1 (difficult) to 10 (easy), how difficult or easy is it for you to believe and embrace the perfect love God has for you?
4. Write out the scripture or scriptures from this chapter that most clearly remind you of God's love for you.

Prayer ===

Let's pray together.

Father, I believe that You have loved me with an ever-lasting love. And I believe that Your deep, unending love is the source of my freedom. I can live with permission today because You loved me before I was born; You have loved me in every moment since; and I have confidence that You will never stop loving me. I am fully Yours. Amen.

SIX

PERMISSION TO GROW SPIRITUALLY

But grow in the grace and knowledge of
our Lord and Savior Jesus Christ.

2 PETER 3:18

DURING ONE OF MY ALL-NIGHTERS AS A PRE-DENTAL UNDER-
grad at Georgia Southern, I was studying with my study buddy, Yasmine. She was an extremely focused student and could easily worry about every little thing because of her desire to do well. It was already about 6:00 a.m., and we had to go in to take an organic chemistry exam at 8:00 a.m. We had stayed up all night trying to read about ten chapters, which was humanly impossible. We decided to just lie down and close our eyes for an hour.

As we were lying there, Yasmine said, "Jackie, what if there is a question on the test about the one chapter of the ten we didn't get to?" We both jumped up with extreme fear, simply at the thought of missing one question. We stayed up the rest of the morning reading that chapter because missing one question was failure in our eyes.

On the outside, everything seemed perfect. I was smart, attractive, and active in church. I had dear friends, a boyfriend, and a family I loved. But on the inside, my hurts and insecurities were raging. The daddy wound that I suffered as a little girl when my dad moved back to his home country of Ghana was still tender. And while I appeared poised and confident, I desperately needed the affirmation of others. As someone who wasn't yet living authentically, I thought I *needed* to achieve—okay, *overachieve*—academically to feel accepted. If I was the best and the brightest, then the hurts I'd endured in my childhood would be healed and I'd finally receive the affirmation I so desperately needed from others.

ONE QUESTION CHANGED IT ALL

Before Yasmine and I ever got the results of our tests—which we ultimately both passed—I called my mom for support. I was crying about how I was not prepared for a test and how I had so much anxiety.

Her reaction, however, disappointed me.

She literally said to me, "Bye, Jackie! Call me back when you find my real daughter again!"

I was a mess.

I was striving in my own strength, all while stamping Jesus' name on it as if He had led me to live this way.

Graciously, though, God had not abandoned me.

One day during my second semester of college, I was walking across campus. School had just resumed after Christmas break, and I went back sporting several of my new outfits. I had a new boo, who I'll call Matt, and I was killing it in the world of academia. I was looking good and feeling great about life.

In the midst of this walk of pride, God stopped me in my tracks with a question. He said, "Jackie, what do you want to be known for?"

I tried to respond with a quick remark. *God, I want people to know how much I love you!* God didn't say another word in that moment, but He disrupted my life in a profound way with that question. It forced me into one of my deepest seasons of intimacy with the Father.

"Jackie, what do you want to be known for?"

In that life-altering moment, I knew in my deep places that even more than I wanted to achieve academically, I wanted to be known as a carrier of Christ, because it is the only identifier that has lasting effects. This decision brought about a huge shift in the way I did *everything*. Although I certainly couldn't have articulated it at the time, I now know that this was the place where I made a huge leap in my permission journey. I hesitate to say it was the start, because I firmly believe that from the time we take our first breath, through the hills and valleys of counterfeit living, our sovereign Lord is using all of it to conform us into the precise and full version of who He created us to be from the beginning. This question from God helped me become a much better partner with the Lord.

Grappling with this helped me to rise above the temporal opinions of others and to access the true core of who I was created to be. Have you ever thought about how you would answer this question?

Sister, what do you want to be known for?

The weight of this question brought about a new priority for so many things in my world. As I wrestled with it daily, I was growing in my ability to clearly hear the voice and instruction of the Lord. I recognized that without His leading I would falter, slipping back into a life dominated by the views and opinions of others. I began to allow God to sharpen my ear. I asked His permission and wisdom regarding everything.

God, what do you want me to wear?

Is it okay to go here?

What do you want me to eat?

As I listened for God's voice, I was aware of the testimony of the apostle Paul, in his letter to the church in Corinth: "'I have the right to do anything,' you say—but not everything is beneficial. 'I have the right to do anything'—but not everything is constructive" (1 Corinthians 10:23). I understood this freedom and certainly avoided anything that wasn't beneficial or constructive. That was baseline. But beyond that, I was eager to hear God's voice leading me, daily, in the smallest of choices. It was His voice in the small choices that was becoming a guardrail, ensuring that I lived my life as He truly designed me to live it.

When I tell you nothing was off-limits, I mean nothing. He began to transform the way I studied. I remember, while enrolled in a parasitology class, asking God to show me how to write Him a love letter on this subject on my next test. Sounds crazy, right? But that's how intentional I had become about inviting God into every part of my life. I allowed Him to be the heartbeat of everything, even my study of parasites. I was on fire for God, and in this season He was giving me permission to be the Jackie He had created me to be.

When God invites you to live a life of freedom, He doesn't expect you to find your own way! And not only does He not expect you to figure out how to live freely, He offers you four pillars of support on which you can build your new life. These four pillars are prayer, the Word, obedience, and faith.

I'm going to share how God erected each of these pillars in my life so that you can catch a glimpse of the life of freedom. And I'll also offer some practical tips so that if you're at the front end of your discipleship journey, if you're new to walking with Jesus, you can find your way as well.

GOD MADE ME A WOMAN OF PRAYER

I recall sitting in my room for hours, worshiping in the presence of the Lord. I offered God everything. In my closet, deciding what to wear for the day, I'd ask God, "Red shirt or blue one?" And I'd begin to notice which one I had a sense of peace about. What was happening was God was training my ear to hear His voice in prayer. He was teaching me that when I had a sense of peace, I could trust I was hearing His voice. And when that peace was disrupted, when I felt like I was forcing something, it probably wasn't the way in which He wanted me to walk.

As a result, I've become a big "peace follower," trusting that in my conversation with God, His Holy Spirit is faithful to help me interpret His voice.

I prayed.

BE A WOMAN OF PRAYER

Rejoice always, pray continually, give thanks in all circumstances; for this is God's will for you in Christ Jesus.

1 THESSALONIANS 5:16–18

I like to call prayer "the dressing room." That's because it's a place where you can take off all the layers you've put on to make you feel cute—the clothes, the undergarments, the accessories, and even the makeup—and strip down to the real version of you. While standing naked in the presence of the Almighty might sound intimidating, I want you to hear me: When you come close to the Lord in this way, He doesn't desire to be known only as Almighty; He wants to reveal Himself as *Abba*, your good and safe Father. The dressing room of prayer is a safe place, as you abide with your Abba.

Imagine yourself standing in front of a full-length mirror. (Stay focused; don't get distracted by focusing on the things you don't like about your body!) If you're Eve in the garden of Eden, this is where you take off the fig leaves—which, you'll remember, weren't God's design at all. That covering up was a result of the fall. When you're able to look into this mirror, you can be entirely vulnerable in God's presence. It's the place to uncover the hurts you've never shown anyone. To examine how scars are healing. To notice any new injuries. The dressing room of prayer is a space for examination, reflection, and assessment. But it's also more. It's where true transformation occurs.

Here you make the choice to be vulnerable, and the Lord is able to minister and heal those places that you keep covered in front of others. Even though some of us have been taught that uncovering ourselves, showing emotion, and admitting we need help are signs of weakness. In prayer we learn that these actions are exactly where God meets us. And what I love is that although you may have walked into the dressing room clothed in shame, after this disrobing and healing that the Lord administers to you, you are able to walk out clothed in the brand-new clothes of dignity. You exchange the garments of insecurity with those of sureness in Christ. He takes off the garment of heaviness and clothes you with joy. There is no dressing room like that of prayer. People walk in sick but leave dressed in wholeness! He never leaves us uncovered when we come to Him!

God is inviting you to discover your true essence. So when you choose to be vulnerable in prayer, you're going to get sneak peeks of her. As you begin to live authentically before God—even before you test-drive your new self in front of others—you'll start to notice those authentic parts of yourself that have been covered.

Who is she?

Where did she come from?

Can I really say that out loud?

Can I really embrace the real me I'm discovering?

In prayer there's room to be in conversation with your true self before test-driving her out in the world.

If prayer is new to you, I want to encourage you to let your prayer life unfold in a natural progression. That means start slow. I'm not sending you into that prayer chamber and insisting you talk to God for an hour. Ease into the relationship.

God Hears You.

This is the confidence we have in approaching God: that if we ask anything according to his will, he hears us.
—1 JOHN 5:14

When a child learns to walk, they wobble. They stumble. They fall. They take a few steps and then retreat into the safe arms of their mommy or daddy.

Perhaps you'll start your prayer journey by writing a simple one-sentence prayer in a journal.

God, You are a Father who is good!

I'm sorry for my sin.

Thank You for meeting my needs today.

Please help me in my marriage.

Or you might start by committing to spend five minutes with the Lord a few times a week.

One thing that is sure to happen as you start to spend any amount of time with the Lord is that your appetite for Him will grow. You're that little baby who awkwardly lifts herself from a crawl to a standing position. Then she waddles for a few steps and tumbles to the ground. Then she starts again.

And as she becomes sure in her steps, she learns to cross the whole room. As confidence grows, she runs.

Allow your appetite for prayer to grow. Don't force it. God is patient and kind. He's enjoying every moment of your time with Him.

The woman living with permission, the woman who's making choices to be the authentic person God made her to be, is a woman of prayer. You simply decide to daily converse with the Lord and invite His guidance into every area of your life. Spending time in the Word helps tremendously with discerning God's voice more clearly and makes prayer even more rewarding.

Let's look at studying the Word.

STUDYING THE BIBLE

God also gave me a hunger for His Word. As I was growing up in church, I had *heard* the Scriptures proclaimed, and I'd even read the Word for myself. But a few years after God had so powerfully captured my attention, during dental school, He invited me to go to a whole new level in feasting on His Word.

My friends and I were studying a book from Zondervan called *The Story*, which was the Bible written in story form. And through that study, God was unlocking His Word for me. He used it to break my fear that the Bible was daunting and unapproachable. As we walked through Scripture, the mysteries of God's Word were being made clear. I was discovering all kinds of good stuff I'd never noticed before. But what I loved most was that I was seeing how principles I saw in Jesus' life were helpful for my everyday life. My friends and I also studied books from a pastor named David Platt, which walked us through God's Word and challenged us to practice radical obedience to what we were discovering.

When I started reading Scripture on my own, I'd keep it simple by following a Bible-reading plan in the back of my Bible. It would tell me what verses to read on a certain day, and I'd do it. If I was told to read the first chapter of Genesis, I read the first chapter of Genesis. No showing off. No mystery on where to start. No reading ahead for extra credit. And—just like starting small in prayer—that grew in me an appetite for more.

Every day that I was able to add another check mark by the date I had completed a reading was such a highlight for me. It wasn't mundane or legalistic. I was excited that I was learning consistency in my relationship with the Lord and seeing the benefits of that time with Him. I was clearer about what God desired of me than I had ever been. I prayed for God to help me grow a love for the Word, because I had tried to accomplish it for a long time in my own efforts. It used to be so hard to just get started. But one step and one day at a time, I became a lover of the Word.

BE A WOMAN OF THE WORD

For the word of God is alive and active. Sharper than any double-edged sword, it penetrates even to

dividing soul and spirit, joints and marrow; it judges
the thoughts and attitudes of the heart.

HEBREWS 4:12

The second pillar for living a life of permission is being a
woman who feasts on the written Word of God that's recorded
in the Bible. Sometimes when women commit to getting into
God's Word in a serious way, they want to do it just right. They
want to be reading the right Bible translation. They want to
start in just the right chapter and verse. They want to read just
the right amount each day. And I get it.

If that's you, I want to say, "Breathe." God's got you. And I
want to just share two guides to help you as you begin.

First, I encourage you to start your study in the New
Testament. Roughly the first 75 percent of the Christian Bible is
the Old Testament, and the New Testament is about the remaining 25 percent. The New Testament is where you're going to
encounter Jesus in the most tangible way. Specifically, I encourage you to start with one of the stories of Jesus' life, called a
gospel. These are the books of Matthew, Mark, Luke, and John.

When we read Scripture, we are noticing how Jesus lived
so that we can live as His faithful followers. As we watch Him
interact with skeptics, believers, people in authority, people
who were disfigured, and people who were blind, we learn
how God is inviting us to move through the world today. Just
as Jesus taught, encouraged, challenged, and loved unconditionally in the first century, He engages with us in those same
ways today!

Second, I want to share the piece of wisdom that has guided me in my own study of Scripture. *Read the Word until the Word reads you.* We read Scripture until it speaks to us. Until it grabs us. Until something in that passage informs the life we're living. It's not about reading a textbook and storing the information in your memory banks. It's about *letting God's Word speak to you.*

Some days you might read several paragraphs before something particular captures your attention in a meaningful way. Other days, you'll read one word—maybe "peace"!—and you'll be done. You'll be done because you know that the word was meant for you. You know that God was speaking to your heart, your situation, revealing His desire to you through that word. And that doesn't mean that you slam the book shut and call it a day. You savor that word. You respond to it by talking to God. You might journal what it means in your situation. You might find the word in the concordance or index in the back of your Bible and see what it means in other parts of the Bible.

When there's something that jumps off the page, when there's something that causes you to reflect on your situation or your walk with God, that's a win. When you're reading a passage of Scripture—possibly one that's familiar—and a passage comes alive in a fresh way, that's called a "rhema word." It's as if the Holy Spirit animates God's Word in a fresh way in your heart. Then ask yourself questions.

What does this mean to me?

How does this change me?

How is God calling me to respond?

Read the Bible until the Bible reads you.

The woman living with permission is a woman of the Word. I often make a practice that if I read about a promise, or the way that Jesus lives that I desire to live, I pray that particular part of the Word over my life. Praying the Word helps to add language to your prayer life. Be sure to write prayers based on what you read and declare with your mouth things you desire to show up in your life.

Let's pray!

 Prayer Prompt

God, I long to be firmly rooted in Your Word. Reveal Yourself and Your instruction to me.

GOD MADE ME A WOMAN OF OBEDIENCE

In that season when God was changing me, I was willing—and so *eager*—to release anything that wasn't of God. I didn't want to be a part of anything that wasn't endorsed by His gift of peace. And in that process, He was teaching me radical obedience.

One of the places God was asking for obedience was in my professional journey. My mom and my grandmama were so proud that I was preparing to attend dental school after college. But as God was offering me permission to be who He made me to be, I was *giving God permission* to take away anything that wasn't from Him. I even laid *dentistry* on the altar. If God wasn't leading me into dentistry, I didn't want to be there. In fact, I had gotten to the point where I recognized that there was no job I was unwilling to do as long as it satisfied Him. I was wide open to whatever His will was. If He desired me to collect trash or go to the moon, I really wanted His way only!

Because obedience is so intimately tied to hearing and responding to God's voice, I wanted to make sure I was hearing God's voice in prayer. When I became aware that I was relying on my mom's counsel, I decided to take a two-week break from talking to my mom—who was and is my very best friend—to be sure I was hearing God's voice as I considered my path toward dentistry. Although I hadn't realized it, the voices and opinions of others had been my guide for a long time. But because I was so intent on hearing and obeying God, I was obedient to silence all other voices.

I had peace about moving forward. Due to a low entrance exam test score, there was a very real chance that I wasn't going to be accepted to dental school at all. On the day I showed up for my interview at *the one school* where I'd applied, I was truly open to His answer being that dentistry was not what He wanted.

On the morning of that interview, God gave me a clear word. He told me that my future of becoming Dr. Jacqueline

Gyamfi was all up to Him. He let me know that if He decided I would be accepted into dental school, then there was nothing on this earth that could stop that word from being established. Just a few days after my interview, I received the call to inform me that I was selected to be one of seventy students to comprise the 2010 dental class at the Medical College of Georgia.

The scripture God gave to me at that time was Joshua 1:7, "Be strong and very courageous. Be careful to *obey* all the instructions Moses gave you. Do not deviate from them, turning either to the right or to the left. Then you will be *successful in everything* you do" (NLT, emphasis added). Through this verse God taught me what true godly success is: living a life of obedience to Him.

One day I said, "Okay God, so what is success?" He said, "Success is living a life of obedience to me." He was teaching me that success isn't determined by the world's values. Success is *obedience*. I recognized that living a successful life was more equivalent to obedience than it was to titles, levels of income, or grades. I began to gain freedom. I stopped striving for things and began striving to obey at all costs.

God Guides You with His Word

Your word is a lamp for my feet, a light on my path.
—PSALM 119:105

I transformed from a person who, at this point in my life, was satisfied by making As, into a person who was satisfied by fully obeying God.

BEING A WOMAN OF OBEDIENCE

Therefore everyone who hears these words of mine and puts them into practice is like a wise man who built his house on the rock.

—MATTHEW 7:24

"I'm going to fast. I'm going to pray. I'm going to give God $100,000."

While that sounds like a pretty nice offer, even a sacrificial one, it might not be what God's after. In the Old Testament Samuel declared to Saul, "Does the LORD delight in burnt offerings and sacrifices as much as in obeying the LORD? To obey is better than sacrifice" (1 Samuel 15:22).

Too often we behave as if we can perform our way into God's good graces. So we make a big show of giving up food by fasting. Or we might even sacrifice financially to give money to God. But what if that's not what He was asking for? What if God had said, "I want two minutes of your time"? To obey, said Samuel, to do what God is asking of you, is better, in God's eyes, than your big, showy sacrifice.

I can almost hear God whispering: "If you would just listen to my voice and obey, you'll find yourself in alignment with my will. Obedience is everything that I desire for you. So when you obey, I'll protect you. I'll care for you."

When you obey, you won't find yourself in bedrooms I didn't call you to.

When you obey, you won't find yourself in jobs I didn't call you to.

When you obey, you'll experience all I have for you.

There's this special provision that accompanies obedience. When we obey, we experience what God has for us. That's not true when we go our own way.

As we learn to be women of obedience, we *want* to obey. And we begin to seek God's voice so that we *can* obey. Let's determine, together, that when we hear God's instruction we *will* obey.

God, do you want me in this church?

God, do you want me in this relationship?

God, do you want me in this job?

And when we do this, our yes and our no align with God's yes and no. That's obedience. The meaning of *obedience* in the Old Testament is "to hear."[2] When a friend of mine was growing up, and she and her siblings failed to obey their parents, their mom or dad would say, "I guess you didn't *hear* me!" When we hear God's voice, we are called to *obey*.

Too often, though, we make it more difficult than that. When we're trying to wiggle out of obedience, we complicate what is simple.

Think about the child who obeys his or her parent. When you invite him to the table, he comes to the table. When you tell her to go to school, she goes to school. When you ask them to stop fighting, they stop. And a Father who is good is inviting you into that kind of simple obedience, from the heart.

And when you give God your yes, He'll lead you to the next door. And when you offer Him your next yes, He'll lead you through that door and to the next. Following God is as simple as agreeing with His yes.

But to keep it real, just because it's simple doesn't mean you'll get it right every time. Like that little child learning to walk, you'll stumble. You'll topple over. Obedience is the same. You have to *practice* it. And Sis, it's worth it.

When God was teaching me how to practice obedience, I'd get up every morning and pray, "God, I want to learn how to hear your voice." Now, it's about to get real here. I had just started dating this guy that I liked *a lot.* For context, he is the guy I ended up marrying. But to help you see how important obedience was in the beginning stages of my relationship with Travis, at the same time I was also at a pivotal point in my growing relationship with the Lord. And there were times when Travis would ask me to come to an event, or do a specific activity, and I still had to ask God for His guidance as to whether it was the right thing to do. I knew Travis was right for me, but that didn't exempt me from inviting God's instructions into the details of how I lived out relationship with Him.

I encourage you to start listening for God's voice speaking to you. My mom used to have this saying: "Jackie, where peace stops, you stop." Where peace stops, you stop. She was saying that when I no longer had a sense of peace—about a relationship, about a decision, about a purchase, about a choice—then I should stop.

So I was inviting God into the smallest decisions of my day. Salad or steak, Lord? Water or tea? Go out with my friends or stay home? And if I didn't have peace, I wouldn't go.

Peace? Go.

No peace? Stop.

Learning to live this way is definitely a process! So the Lord would nudge me, "Pick up that piece of trash." I'd rationalize, "That's not God's voice. That's not God." But as I walked on, I'd notice that I didn't have peace anymore. So, grudgingly, I'd go back and pick up that trash. Guess what? Peace. When I followed God's instruction, I'd find peace again.

Let me make one point of clarification: peace is not synonymous with comfort. Many times the Lord nudged me to do something, and my heart would begin to race. I would think of all the things that could go wrong. I would second-guess.

God Created You to Obey Him.

If you love me, keep my commands.
—JOHN 14:15

This is not a lack of peace. This is fear, doubting, and anxiety. You have to get clear on this difference. Many of the things you will do for God in obedience will be scary, but they won't rob you of that deep inner peace. And when you obey despite the outcome, you will feel this great sense of fulfillment. This, my sister, is the confirmation of peace and you being bold enough to do it, even if you had to do it afraid!

The woman living with permission is a woman of obedience.

FAITH I DIDN'T ASK FOR

Throughout this pivotal season when God was teaching me how to live with permission, He was building an unshakable faith inside me. As He invited me to release the ways of the world, He also gave me faith to trust that what He had for me was even better than what I could orchestrate for myself.

Earlier in the book I mentioned Matt, the guy I dated for most of my undergrad years. He wasn't a bad guy. In fact, everyone who knew him would confirm that he was a really good guy. But he didn't challenge me to live above the place I already existed in God. All of the challenges came from me. The desire to live pure came from me. The desire to go deeper in God came from me. Matt was fully satisfied with a comfortable Jackie, so I already knew that he would not be the kind of guy who could lead me in my future.

I wrestled many times while standing at the altar at church. "God, if I leave his life, how will Matt ever get to know you better? How will he ever reach the full potential for his life?" Because you all missed the fact that I was his Lord and Savior Jackie Gyamfi, right?! But my junior year, with the faith that God had grown in me, I was finally able to let Matt go for good.

It takes faith to end a relationship that's "good enough" but isn't God's best for you. It takes faith to refuse the amazing job you've been offered when you don't have God's peace about it. It takes faith to choose God's way when the people around you disapprove.

We exercise faith in God when we obey what we've heard from Him, trusting in what God spoke to Isaiah: "For my thoughts are not your thoughts, neither are your ways my ways" (Isaiah 55:8). And God continued, "As the heavens are higher than the earth, so are my ways higher than your ways and my thoughts than your thoughts" (v. 9). We exercise faith when we live obediently because we're convinced that God's ways are not just right but better than ours.

What that developing faith looked like in my life was being willing to let go of my desires so I could find out what God was actually speaking to me. And God was giving me the courage to say yes in faith. On my journey, and I suspect on yours, God gives many opportunities to exercise faith. After we married, Travis and I found out we were pregnant with our first child during my senior year of dental school. To say we were excited would be an understatement.

In my twentieth week of pregnancy, I went in for my anatomy scan. We had planned to ask the doctor reading the sonogram to share the gender of the baby in preparation for our gender reveal that weekend. During my anatomy scan, it was clear that something was very wrong. The sonographer wasn't able to give me any information. I noticed that when my OB came into the room, she was more concerned with the scan than with me. I called her by her name and asked what was going on. She instructed me to call my mom and tell her to get back to the hospital. My cervix was wide open, which allowed my amniotic bag to bulge down through the opening. I was immediately admitted into the hospital.

It was becoming clear that my condition was extremely severe. This was my first baby! I thought to myself, *Lord, what is happening?!* We made it to my room, and I asked the nurse, "So I know the doctor said I had to be admitted, but do you know how long I will be here? Will this be a few days or weeks?" She was so gracious when she responded. "You may want your family to bring you all the things you love to pass the time. You could be in here for several weeks!" Talk about being hit with the unexpected.

That night we decided to go ahead and open the envelope that held the gender of our baby. We were pregnant with a baby boy we had already decided to name David Jace Greene. David, because that is the name of one of Travis's favorite Bible characters, and he has several impactful mentors with this name. Jace was the name of one of my dental school friend's sons. When I found out its meaning, I was sold. Jace means "Healer" and "The Lord is my salvation."

We were in for the fight of our lives. After a consult with a high-risk obstetrician, we all came together to pray and decide what we felt God was leading us to do. I pray that you are grasping the reality of where we were as parents. I went in for a doctor's appointment expecting to receive the envelope for my gender reveal. Instead, I was lying in a hospital bed being told that they would put me to sleep to do a procedure, and I could only hope my child would still be alive when I woke up. Talk about moments of desperation. We decided, after praying, that we felt peace about moving forward with the procedure.

Before they wheeled me back to the operating room,

my family surrounded my bed, along with the high-risk OB who would be performing the procedure. I recall seeing her weep as my family prayed down the manifested presence of God. We were sure that our baby boy was in God's hands, and that there was no safer place he could be! We gave God our complete trust. I went into surgery and awakened to the news that, although it was a tough procedure, they were able to complete it successfully! My baby boy was doing great, and I was so grateful!

But the fight for his life wasn't over! The following week we received even worse news. Despite the procedure my water still ended up breaking. This dealt a heavy blow to our faith. Daily the doctors told us how much more fluid had been lost and how the viability of my pregnancy was becoming increasingly uncertain. After weeks of this, when my fluid level had passed the critical mark, we experienced a miracle. Within one day the levels began to rebuild, and the doctors said this could only be possible if my amniotic sac somehow resealed.

Travis and I thanked God for the miracle, but each of the sixty-three days was super challenging for our faith. We had to fight to remember the words of faith that had been uttered regarding my pregnancy: "Jackie shall birth a healthy baby boy!" In the face of daily reports confirming how unlikely the viability of this pregnancy was, Jace had made it to twenty-eight weeks and one day, and they could no longer stop the contractions. So my doctor decided to perform an emergency C-section and bring David Jace on into the world!

At 5:59 a.m. on May 27, 2014, after sixty-three days of bed

rest, our little fighter was born. He was immediately taken to the neonatal intensive care unit. They placed him on a ventilator for just a few hours and then removed it because they saw he was able to breathe on his own.

After sixty-one additional days of Jace being hospitalized, we left the hospital holding our little miracle! As I held him, I was still holding on to the promise that God gave me as I lay in the hospital bed perplexed as to why all these things had suddenly happened. God had said to me, "Jackie, Jace will have no remnants of prematurity!" I stood on this promise through every dark day of the journey. I was sure that God was a keeper of His word.

BEING A WOMAN OF FAITH

Now faith is confidence in what we hope for and assurance about what we do not see.

HEBREWS 11:1

The woman of faith trusts God more than she trusts herself. Before she can ever believe in herself, she has to believe in God.

Faith is like a muscle. When you exercise it, you gain more. Sometimes people *want* faith, but they're not willing to practice and build faith. They're not willing to exercise it.

It's like the unhealthy person who magically wants to have a good, healthy diet. Well, that begins with nibbling on a carrot. Crunching a piece of broccoli. Savoring an apple. And the more you eat those bites of healthy food, the more you grow an appetite for them. You grow a lifestyle.

Today I am far enough into this permission journey that pleasing people simply doesn't satisfy. I used to be easily swayed by the whims of people and who they wanted me to be. But today that no longer satisfies me since I've built up an appetite for faith in God. Don't get me wrong; sometimes I'm still inclined to be a people pleaser and it still takes lots of diligence and intentionality, but the junk food that the world has to offer just won't do.

What has your junk food been? Where have you settled for consuming what the world offers? God is offering you something so much better and I pray that, one bite at a time, you'll begin to feast on what truly satisfies.

In a letter to Christians in Rome, the apostle Paul

God Gives You Faith.

For I say, through the grace given to me, to everyone who is among you, not to think of himself more highly than he ought to think, but to think soberly, as God has dealt to each one a measure of faith.
—ROMANS 12:3 NKJV

reminded them, and us, that "faith comes from hearing the message, and the message is heard through the word about Christ" (Romans 10:17). You can't develop faith, you can't build it, in isolation. Center yourself in a community of strong fellowship. Seek out a church body with hearty teaching and preaching. Find a people who are passionate about being rooted in the truth of the Bible. Begin serving there. Begin fellowshipping there. Begin growing there. By investing in this way of life, you'll be in a position to live powerfully by faith.

When I meet a new woman, one of the ways I discern whether she is living by faith is by her language. I hear it in her speech. Women who live by faith watch what comes out of their mouths. They don't allow just any words to pass their lips.

For example, the other day I heard a woman say, "I don't know what's going to happen to me." It sounds like a small thing, right? But the woman of faith says, "If I hit a hard moment, I know that God is with me." Her language reveals her *faith* even in rough patches. "I can't see what's next, but I know the One who can." "This doesn't make sense, but I am still trusting God." Yes, life happens to us all. But the way a woman of faith interprets her circumstances reveals her faith.

There's more. And as you develop an ear for it, you'll begin to hear it. She speaks well of others. She speaks well of herself. Her speech is sprinkled with boldness. *The woman who is living in the freedom God gives her is living by faith.*

When you choose to embrace the permission God has given you, you know that there is nothing you did to earn it. And as you walk in that permission, there's nothing you need to do to keep it. You don't have to keep proving yourself to God or other people. What you can do, though, to stay rooted in the reality of your identity as God's beloved, is to strengthen in yourself the four pillars of permission living: prayer, Scripture, obedience, and faith.

I can't emphasize enough how much these four pillars are going to empower you to have a living relationship with God. If that's what you want, if you're hungry to know Him and speak with Him and hear from Him, these pillars will equip you for that kind of vibrant faith.

═══ **Embrace Permission Exercise** ═══

Notice the ways that you've utilized these four important tools before today:

- Prayer
- God's Word
- Obedience
- Faith

1. As you listen for God's voice welcoming you to grow in these four areas, what are you hearing?
2. What are practical ways that you can commit to these practices?

Hint: Start small. That is going to be the big win.

═══════════════════ **Prayer** ═══

Let's pray together.

Father, I am eager to grow in my relationship with You. So I commit myself to the practice of prayer, grateful to converse with You. Open my heart and mind as I study Your Word. Grant me the courage to obey You, even when it's hard. My choice is to follow You in faith! Amen.

SEVEN

PERMISSION TO LIVE INTENTIONALLY

Therefore, if anyone is in Christ, the new creation has come. The old has gone, the new is here!

2 CORINTHIANS 5:17

AS YOU PURPOSE TO LIVE IN THE PERMISSION GOD HAS given you, there are three areas of focus you can choose to become the woman God created you to be:

1. You can choose authenticity.
2. You can choose transparency.
3. You can choose community.

Your living is authentic when you're being yourself— the self God created you to be. Authenticity is the bedrock of what the life of permission is all about. It's not something that happens in isolation. Authenticity begins vertically. We must reference the Designer! Living the authentic life does not begin between ourselves and others. For we are unable to know or declare what is real and authentic until we first consult with the Creator. His are the hands holding the blueprint for how the creation was originally intended to function, which is what allows us to identify and remedy any malfunction or modification to the creation, in light of the original design.

I've seen many fall prey to a hiccup I experienced in my own journey toward authenticity. We too quickly turn outward, horizontally, in our focus. We look out toward the faces of others. We don't spend enough time focused vertically on the relationship between the Designer and the designed!

When we do that, it's as if we're looking to the driver of the vehicle—or the passenger—to see if the car is running as it should be. When in fact that person is limited in the knowledge of *all* that makes the car unique. The best others can offer is their opinion based on their experience. And the danger in trying to build a foundation from those users' opinions is that many cars are created as prototypes, which means there is no reference for their design. And when that car is taken back to its original manufacturer, the level of insight and understanding the designer can offer about that car is mind-blowing.

This is true for our life of authenticity as well. You can identify a woman who has spent intentional time discovering the true essence of who she was fully created to be. It's what you're noticing when you enter a room and encounter a woman who is comfortable in her own skin and being exactly who God intended. And when others encounter *you*, they can sense your authenticity in the way you make eye contact. In the way you carry yourself. In the way you walk into a room. Authenticity means that all cylinders are firing because you're operating the way God designed *you* to function.

Your living is *transparent* when you allow your authenticity to be seen. What was gained in the vertical relationship is communicated horizontally. In living the life of permission, the challenge is to allow your newfound freedom to impact your relationship with others. It's not enough to simply come to know who you are authentically. Because when you have the courage to live transparently, you take living freely to a whole other level! You live transparently before others when you're willing to be vulnerable with those who can be trusted. The transparent woman is willing to be honest, to let down her guard, to uncover what others hide for the sake of being accepted. She refuses to cover up, to pose, to pretend, or to build walls. When others encounter her, they experience *who she really is.*

Like transparency, community also happens in a horizontal space. But rather than being singular—as in another's experience of just you—community is a corporate experience between a body of believers. Women and men who choose to live in community are agreeing to share life by investing in one another and in the world around them. The one who chooses to live her life in community is a blessing to others. And when she's in need, there are people around her who strengthen and support her. The unique gifts and way of being that she brings enhance her community. And what her community offers enhances her life.

AUTHENTICALLY COURTNEY

Courtney grew up with a mother for whom appearances were very important. On school days her mother dressed her in corduroy pants, monogrammed sweaters, and a matching, preppy, monogrammed handbag. On Sundays young Courtney wore shiny black leather shoes, white tights, a pressed and starched dress, and an embroidered headband. What she learned about others is that they were always watching, always judging. And what she learned about herself was that she needed to appear as if she were flawless.

As an adult, Courtney continued to wear the designer clothes and carry the designer bags. The appearance of her outfits, her home, her car—and even her husband and children—let others know that she was *acceptable*.

But appearing acceptable to others didn't satisfy Courtney like she thought it might. And as she began to feel as if there was something missing, she was invited to join a prayer group in her neighborhood. Although she feared it was going to be too churchy, Courtney showed up. And despite the fact that she initially felt awkward, she encountered women who lived in homes like hers but who were on fire about their relationship with God. She sensed in these women a depth she'd been hungering for in her life. And in relationship with them, she began to discover that God had more for her to discover about who He was, who she was, and how He'd uniquely designed her to be a blessing in the world He loved.

When Courtney really began to live in her truest identity, as one who was accepted and beloved by God simply for the reason that He'd made her, she was set free to explore and discover who she was. She was liberated, by God's radical acceptance, to explore the parts of herself she hadn't yet discovered.

As Courtney spent time with God, she came to know

Him as a lover of orphans and widows. As she listened to Him, He reminded her of the ways that she reached out to kids who were outcasts in elementary school, and how she loved visiting with the elderly folks who lived in the nursing home where her great-grandmother lived. As God began to show Courtney that He'd made her to reflect this part of who He was, she invited her husband to consider opening their home to a foster child. A year later, their family was welcoming a three-year-old girl to share their lives for as long as she needed to.

Courtney became the lover of orphans that God had made her to be when He formed her. Another woman who is set free by God to be her authentic self will begin using her voice—speaking from the stage, or singing original songs, or advocating for justice. Another woman who begins to own her permission will sell her large home and find a smaller, more affordable one because she no longer needs others to believe she's doing well in life. None of these women are persuaded at all by others' opinions, because they're so securely identified by God's acceptance that they're free to live authentically.

Authenticity is being who God created you to be. It's this vertical transaction in which you embrace the version of you that is the person God created you to be. Your eyes are on God, and God's eyes are you.

Living a life of authenticity is living a life of freedom. It's like being in a place where you find yourself breathing fresh air, fully open and vulnerable. You're full of expectation, full of joy. Nothing is hidden. Everything in you is facing forward.

You are passionate about the way God made you and you have a sense of purpose. You feel affirmed by the Lord.

One of the key signs of authenticity is that you feel affirmed from within. You don't depend on external validation for your worth. You're sure. You're steady. You're confident.

> **Always Remember: You Are Made to Live Authentically Before God.**
>
> For you created my inmost being; you knit me together in my mother's womb. I praise you because I am fearfully and wonderfully made; your works are wonderful, I know that full well.
> —PSALM 139:13–14

But all this strength doesn't mean that you're a superhero. What it does mean is that when you're faced with challenges, you're equipped to face them differently. For example, when I was living as a counterfeit, when people would say something that bothered me, I'd shove it down. And I'd apply a spiritual veneer, saying, "I'll just take it to the Lord." I'd take the blow and just pray about it, never dealing with the person with whom I had an issue.

But God began to whisper, "No, baby. Go back out there and tell them, 'When you did that, I felt this way.'" And when I started doing that, it made me so much healthier! That's what authenticity does. It says *no* to counterfeit living and challenges you to *remain free!*

Prayer Prompt

Jesus, today I make the choice to be precisely and fully who I was created by You to be. I'm paying attention. Show me.

TAMMY'S AWAKENING

The woman I'm calling Tammy was in one of our earliest Permission Room groups. She was working as a first-grade teacher, where she found some joy, but she would come home and experience loneliness and depression. When we connected after church one week, we agreed to meet up for an early breakfast at IHOP the next day.

As we chatted before ordering, I sensed that Tammy had put up some walls to keep others at a distance. To keep herself from getting hurt again. She let me see some of who she was, the things she couldn't hide, but she wasn't willing to open up about what was really stinging inside her.

That breakfast was the first in a series of occasional meet-ups through the year, when I would gently encourage Tammy to consider beginning therapy as a tool to help her heal. I didn't push her hard. I shared how helpful having sound counsel had been in my own healing, and I encouraged her to consider how God might use it in her life to set her free.

One day, as we grabbed breakfast donuts together, she

surprised me. "Well," she said between bites, "it wasn't as bad as I thought."

"What wasn't?" I asked her

"Therapy," she announced, with a little smile on her face.

I did not see that one coming!

She confessed, "I think my resistance to returning to my early hurts has been keeping me stuck."

Possibly.

As Tammy continued with therapy and as she learned how to spend time with the Lord in her Permission Room group, He opened her eyes to see herself a bit more clearly. And slowly, I began to see those walls she'd erected begin to crumble. I saw her developing friendships with other women and even going out on a few dates. As God worked in Tammy, I saw a beautiful transformation.

I knew that Tammy had been hearing the permission message in our conversations. And she shared with me that she was gradually accepting that she was beloved by God. When we have that security of being firmly rooted in God's love for us, it allows us to see ourselves more clearly.

Before Tammy could ever be transparent with a friend, with me, or with a family member, God had to help her see *herself* clearly first. He had to teach her to be authentic before Him. And when she did, she was able to tiptoe into being transparent with me and then with others.

When I was performing for the eyes of others, I didn't want anyone to see how insecure I really was. So I put on the mask of accomplishment, of confidence, of success. I allowed others to see only what I wanted them to see. But when God gave me permission to live in the freedom of who I really was, I saw my relationships shift. When I began to embrace who I really was (authenticity) and allow others to see it (transparency), all my relationships were enhanced.

Transparency, of course, depends on authenticity first. When you're not in touch with who you really are, then you're not aware of when you're hiding and when you're covering up. But when you choose transparency built on authenticity, you begin to allow the real you to be seen in public spaces: your thoughts, your feelings, your opinions. And you're able to do it because it's a safe thing to do. When you're authentically grounded in the fact that you are beloved by God, you can show others who you really are.

In Tammy's Permission Room group, another woman had shared that she had been verbally abused by her mother as a child. Seeing that woman live transparently opened up the possibility for Tammy that she, too, could live transparently before others. Did the possibility scare Tammy? It sure did. But she also recognized the freedom with which this woman was

You Are Made to Live Transparently in Relationship with Others.

Do not lie to each other, since you have taken off your old self with its practices and have put on the new self, which is being renewed in knowledge in the image of its Creator.
—Colossians 3:9–10

living as she shared her story with others who cared for her. One morning Tammy gathered her courage and shared with her sisters about how her childhood experience had affected her adult life. Later that day Tammy noticed a tangible freedom—that she could feel in her body—that resulted from living transparently.

Living with permission always begins with becoming the authentic version of who God made us to be. And when we live authentically, when we're securely rooted in our identities, we can at last be transparent with others.

THE COMMUNITY THAT SHAPED ME

I arrived at Georgia Southern in August of 2006. My first weekend there, I was privileged to meet the friend circle I would carry with me for my entire college duration. What we came to call The Square was four friends who lived, slept, ate, and churched together. We were inseparable. The Square was Angie, Keshia, Camia, and me—four girls from various backgrounds who were prepared to start college together. We all came with our own sets of baggage and things that would have to be changed along the way. One thing I can say is that from the very beginning of this friend group we established that God was always the main theme. I was seen as the mama of the group. By this time I was all about making good decisions that I would not look back on and regret. I didn't do this perfectly. I still made silly choices from time to time.

Specifically, I remember how my friends and I would pursue God together. It was not uncommon for us to convert our bedrooms or living room into a full-on church service. My friend Keshia is a very anointed prophetic dancer, Angie sings with such a yoke-breaking anointing, and Camia has a sweet anointing for intercession. God often used me during these times to speak words of affirmation and to break down Scripture to nourish us. We returned to these basics many times, especially when we felt we were getting off course. We desired to serve God from a pure place. It was moments like these—when we sat before the Lord with no agenda, and times alone in my room crying out to God—that I truly established my own personal relationship with God.

In addition to the fellowship I enjoyed with The Square, I began attending an on-fire ministry in Statesboro, Georgia, known as Spirit and Truth Worship Center. This setting would provide the backdrop for me to embrace the radical nature of my worship for God and to begin the early stages of recognizing that I had a voice tailor-made for empowering.

This ministry was filled with numerous college kids from a vast array of backgrounds and upbringings. What connected all of us was our love for Christ and a desire to live fully surrendered lives. For my friends and me, this ministry was a huge part of our lives. We attended Sunday service, Bible study, nights of worship, events on campus, trips to other churches, and hermeneutics and homiletics classes. If the doors of that church were open, we were most likely there.

This was the first time in my life when I was exposed to

other believers who loved God and had pursued Him heavily in their youth. I became very close with two young ladies, Cassandra and Tarrah. I was able to glean so much from both of them throughout my time at Georgia Southern. It was always clear that they both believed in the unique gifts God had placed on my life, and they walked alongside me to help uncover these gifts.

Our leader, Pastor J, was the exact same way. I will forever honor this man for the deposit he made in my life. Pastor J always inspired me to just be me. He seemed to have such regard for the things God placed on my heart. He added me to a team of young people that he trained to be ministers and began to prepare me for my future, although I couldn't have imagined I'd ever preach in front of huge audiences.

A few years later, at one of Travis's music engagements after we were married, the pastor of the church where Travis was performing invited us to the green room, behind the stage, to speak a word over us. Beginning with me, he prophesied that I would be brought before the great kings and queens of this world, and that I would declare the truth of God's Word in a very powerful way. At the time, I couldn't have imagined how that would be expressed in my life, but now I *see*! And I return to those holy words in the moments when the enemy is working overtime trying to convince me to doubt my call. I hold tight to the words God spoke to me through that pastor.

I want you to understand that being in community was essential to my becoming the version of myself that God made me to be. It couldn't have happened without my sisters in Christ. It couldn't have happened without my church and pastor. I needed community to be set free and stay free, to live with the freedom God intended.

This still holds true today. My husband, trusted counsel, mentees, and the women of Forward City all play a vital role in who I have continued to become. My current God-selected tribe of women love me, nurture me, affirm me, push me, and continue to sustain the initial work begun when I was a college girl. I am who I am today largely due to the many incredible women I have the pleasure of doing life with.

MADE FOR COMMUNITY

You know how when someone writes something in ALL CAPS it kinda feels like they're shouting at you? I'll scream this from the depths of me:

THE LIFE OF PERMISSION CAN'T BE DONE ALONE!

Was that loud enough? The life of freedom, living a life of permission, simply can't be sustained without community.

Pam the pleaser is a great example. In her tireless efforts to be everything for everybody, the one person she neglected was herself. For Pam's life to change, though, the place she needed to be wasn't the day spa, indulging in self-care. Pam needed to be in fellowship with other believers who knew her and loved her. That's different from volunteering for every committee. That's different from staying into the wee hours of the morning preparing the sanctuary for worship. That's even different from dipping into worship five minutes late and dashing out five minutes before the end of service. Pam needed to know other godly believers and be known by them. That often happens in small groups. It might happen at a women's event. And it can certainly happen by finding another woman with whom you can pray and practice accountability. For Pam to be all that God created her to be, she actually needed to *do* less at church and *be*—be present, be loved, be loving—more.

You need that too. Because if you're a pleaser, you're going to have moments when you're weak. You're going to have moments when you lapse back into the old habits—of comfort, of pleasing, of fear—and when you do, you need the body of Christ. You need the voices of sisters who are going to remind you of who you truly are!

"Hey, you don't act like that anymore. Remember?"

"That's not who you really are."

"That was the counterfeit version of you."

"God has made you *new*."

Members of the body of Christ water and nurture the version of you who's being transformed into the woman God made you to be. They know you. They love you. They speak the same language you speak. They protect you from sliding back into old habits; they have your back.

Without this support, you can expect to fall back into your old ways.

"You're no longer the Pam who pleases. You're powerful Pam!"

Your community is this guardrail of protection around the

work that God is doing in you. And when you begin to veer off the path, they'll steer you back in the right direction. Besides protecting you, they also help you notice and discover new parts of you as they emerge.

A friend who's known you for years notices that you are more confident than you once were.

A sister from church comments that when you walk into a room, you seem more comfortable taking up space, rather than shrinking into the background.

Another mentor observes that the way you're sharing your creative gifts, in new ways, is blessing the church.

Godly Christian community is a gift from God meant to both protect and nurture you. Your community sees who you really are, and they keep you from behaving as if you're anything other than that. You may experience

You Are Made for Community.

But if we walk in the light, as he is in the light, we have fellowship with one another, and the blood of Jesus, his Son, purifies us from all sin.
—1 JOHN 1:7

this kind of holy fellowship among a small group of friends. Or you may join a life group, or small group, at your church. And you may even find this kind of sisterhood as a member of Permission Room. In all kinds of ways, God is so faithful to provide the community we need.

Finally, notice that these acts, protecting and nurturing, aren't a one-way street. One woman who's poured into me when I've been weak is my makeup artist, Kristy! Yes, I'm her pastor. But she's seen me when I haven't been on top of my game. When I was vulnerable. Although she has seen the empowered version of me, she has also delighted in empowering me when I was feeling afraid or hesitant about growth and change. And she did it without judgment.

If you're a woman in leadership, whether a pastor or another type of leader, I know the temptation to look like you have it all together. It can even feel like a way to love your flock, by being strong for them. But it's time to flip that! *You love people as you model what it looks like to be vulnerable, not what it looks like to cover up.* So if you're a leader, identify those safe people around whom you can reveal who you really are, in any given moment.

 Prayer Prompt

Jesus, what woman, or women, are You inviting me to pursue intentionally to develop an authentic and transparent relationship?

GROWING IN PERMISSION

As you think about living with authenticity, transparency, and in community, where's the place that you most need to grow? You don't need to master everything all at once. So ask God which of these three choices is the right next step for you, and then commit to one personal practice that will reinforce your decision to live with authenticity, transparency, or in community. Maybe you'll take a break from wearing makeup, for a minute, to embrace being your authentic self before God and others. Or you might choose to reveal a personal secret to a friend. Or you might decide to join a small group at church. As God leads, just take your *next* step.

And remember the four pillars of permission? They are prayer, Scripture, obedience, and faith. Committing to those four practices is going to strengthen your ability to live authentically, transparently, and in community with others.

As you're living the permission life—claiming the true self God made you to be, day by day, moment by moment— you're making a myriad of choices. And using the filters of authenticity, transparency, and community will help you live faithfully as you make those choices.

=== **Embrace Permission Exercise** ===

As you consider these three choices (authenticity, transparency, community) that support your commitment to live with permission, notice the areas in which you need to grow. Start by noticing where you might have weakness.

Hint: Being specific is going to be more useful than being vague. Listing examples will help you notice these areas today and remember them when you return to them.

- Ways that I'm not yet living with authenticity . . .
- Ways that I'm not yet living with transparency . . .
- Ways that I'm not yet embracing community . . .

Then choose one practical step you can take to live more freely:

a. One way that I can live with more authenticity is . . .
b. One way that I can live with more transparency is . . .
c. One way that I can embrace community is . . .

Prayer

Let's pray together.

Lord, I thank You for equipping me to lead the life You've already granted me permission to live! I commit to live honestly, with authenticity, before You. I commit to live transparently, allowing others to see who I really am. And I commit to investing in the Christian community You provide. In Jesus' name, amen.

EIGHT

PERMISSION TO STEP OUT IN FAITH

The Lord makes firm the steps of the
one who delights in him.

PSALM 37:23

"HEY, SISTERS, I NEED HELP . . ."

A few years back, when I was working part time as a dentist and taking care of our boys, I called together a few friends to join me in what I sensed God was leading me to do.

While I was grateful for all I had, I was ready for a change. I knew God had more for me that I wasn't accessing. I knew it because I was hungry for *more*. I knew it because a pastor had prophesied that one day I'd flourish as a communicator. As I listened to God, I knew He had more for me.

So I invited some close friends to join me for a weekend at an Airbnb, to share with them what I was sensing about God's leading at that time. I was tired of sitting on the gifts God had given me, I explained, and I was eager to just get started. I was ready to stop delaying obedience—to pursue the dreams and visions God had given me—and to finally go for it. So we set out to host our first one-day women's conference. Within two months of our meetup, fueled by their encouragement and support and ideas, I hosted a conference called Exhale, designed to challenge women to live a life of freedom by taking a moment to pull away and just breathe.

If you're imagining the kind of conference you may have attended recently—with professional lighting, paid musicians, skilled camera crews, and carefully orchestrated transitions—please don't imagine that at all. About 150 women gathered at the back of the facility our church had been renting, with very dim lighting and absolutely no glamour or glitz. Planning and executing that conference was my first step. I did the best I could with what I had.

But guess what? That wobbly first step made me believe that I could take another. And then another. And then another.

You've seen the videos parents take of their babies' first steps, right? A sweet little toddler, who's just learned to stand holding on to the couch, will tentatively release his grip and take a step toward his daddy's open arms. You can hear siblings screaming and see grandparents beaming in the background. And we celebrate because we know that once that little guy takes one step, he's eventually going to take five steps. And then ten. And before you know it, he's competing on the world stage in the Olympics, running a 100-yard dash. And as he crosses the finish line, the mama who's watching him from the bleachers in that faraway country *remembers* his first wobbly step. The first step is what launches the whole journey.

IT BEGINS WITH A SINGLE STEP

My first step toward living with permission in the area of women's ministry was hosting the Exhale conference. *And I'm convinced that the first step is the most powerful step!* It's what launches you on the journey into which God is leading you.

So I want you to see what that first step looked like in the lives of a few women I know.

God called Courtney out of counterfeit living to live more authentically before Him. And as she spent time with God and was reminded of the precise way He had created her—with a love for those on the world's margins—Courtney heard God calling her to welcome a child into her family's home. And that's kind of big, right? And for her, it felt pretty daunting. But guess what? That big thing began with a single step. As Courtney talked with others who provided foster care, and as she researched the process, she and her husband signed up to take a Saturday morning workshop for people who were interested in becoming foster parents. That was it. Courtney's first step to live in the freedom God had for her was to sign up, show up, eat some donuts, and listen. The journey into a life of freedom begins with just one step.

Tammy's first step into freedom also felt a little challenging. The way she'd survived for years was to armor up and erect walls to guard herself from being hurt again. But as she got little glimpses of what freedom might look like, as she began to have conversations with other survivors, she knew that one of the tools God wanted to use in her healing was therapy. After asking a friend she trusted to recommend a counselor who might be a good fit for her, Tammy's first step was to leave a phone message requesting an appointment. It took all of thirty seconds for her to make the request and leave her name and number.

Courageous first steps will look different in the life of every uniquely designed woman. So while God called Comfortable Courtney to step into serving, He actually called Pleasing Pam to step *away* from serving for a season! Because for Pam to live in freedom, she needed to be nourished by the body of believers. She needed to be fully present in worship, without thinking about finding a broom to sweep up loose Cheerios she saw on the floor beside a toddler. She needed to participate in a small group where she could be deeply known by sisters and brothers who cared for her. So Pam's first step into freedom was to make plans to see a movie with another single mama from that small group.

Frieda's first step was to ask a friend to be her accountability partner, checking in to make sure she was putting at least five hours a week into writing.

And Unique signed up for one class at the local community college to begin accruing the credits she needed to finally earn her degree. The journey into a life of freedom begins with just one step.

James wrote, "Do not merely listen to the word, and so deceive yourselves. Do what it says" (James 1:22). That's pretty plain, isn't it? When James looked at the early church, he recognized the human temptation to believe the right thing without putting it into action. It was a temptation in the first century, and today we face that same temptation. When women participate in Permission Room, or Permission World, or our Permission Conference, my team and I pour

God's *truth* into them. They receive what Peter called the kind of "pure spiritual milk" that babies crave (1 Peter 2:2).

But that nutrition isn't for us to grow fat! No, it's meant to be fuel to propel us into a life of freedom. And it's critically important, to me and to our team, that women understand that. *What we know is meant to fuel what we do.* As our eyes are opened to the liberating life of permission, the truth we discover is meant to change the way we behave. And any inspiration you've found in these pages is meant to propel you to *action.*

Prayer Prompt

God, let the truth about who You are transform my living!

WHAT WE KNOW ABOUT TAKING OUR FIRST STEP INTO FREEDOM

I thank God for the privilege of seeing countless women take their first steps into a life of freedom. I never cease to be amazed by the endless creativity of God—both in the way that He made each of these women unique and in how His permission has been, and continues to be, expressed in their lives. And as I've watched these women step into freedom, I've noticed three common factors I want to share with you. My hope is that, as you seek God's leading in your own life, these will help you to recognize the way He may be leading *you.*

Common Factor #1: Your first step in the permission journey is unique to you, determined by your precise design.

Your custom design is different from mine. It's different from your cousin's. It's different from your neighbor's. So your first step into permission living is going to be unique to you. If God designed you to be a creator, your first step might be to purchase a sketchbook. If God made you to be an entrepreneur, your first step might be to sign up for a business course. If God created you to serve those who are vulnerable, your first step might be volunteering for a few hours at a local nonprofit.

After hearing me teach that hurt people hurt people, one woman saw her situation in a whole new light. She texted a message of forgiveness to the person who'd wounded her years before. And as she experienced freedom, she purposed to set someone else free. One woman who'd been trudging along for years in a job she hated took the step of filling out a job application for a position more suited to her gifts and passions. One woman who hadn't lifted a paintbrush in decades signed up for a painting class and began to do the thing God made her to do. Your first step is going to be custom fit to who God made you to be.

Common Factor #2: Your first step in the permission journey will likely involve a degree of risk or discomfort.

When I accepted God's invitation to put on the Exhale conference, it involved a degree of risk. What if I failed? What if no one showed up? What if I choked? What God was inviting me to do took me out of my comfort zone and into a new place where I had to trust Him. And that's what I see in the lives of countless women who've accepted God's invitation to live with permission. They are brave and bold to step into an area in which they're not yet comfortable.

One woman took the courageous step of taking a course to be trained to fly a plane! (Both risk *and* discomfort!) One woman began writing poetry and sharing it with others on Facebook. One woman returned to night school—after she finished her day job—to earn her degree in nursing. One woman said goodbye to her steady, boring, well-paying job for a nonprofit to buy a business about which she was truly passionate. And another woman, an immigrant who had been cleaning houses, committed herself to improving her command of the English language so that she would be prepared to secure the job she really wanted in the food service industry. Each woman took a step into something that required courage!

Common Factor #3: Your first step in the permission journey leads you out of bondage and into freedom.

At the time I said yes to hosting Exhale, no one would have looked at my life and thought that I was living in bondage. I was happy to be Travis's wife and grateful to be rearing our sons. But if I'd refused God's invitation to use all that He had put inside me, I would have been living in bondage to a life that was less than what God created for me—even though it was, and is, a great life! Your bondage—to a bad relationship, or to a death-dealing job, or to a controlling addiction—might look more like bondage than mine did. But anything less than the life of flourishing that God created us for is a kind of bondage.

One woman showed up at her first meeting of Alcoholics Anonymous. Another woman made the decision to practice celibacy when a man she'd been dating was unwilling to make a commitment to her. One woman, whose doctor had cautioned her about the way her habits were impacting her health, joined a neighborhood walking group. And one older woman with poor balance, whose pride had kept her from using a walker, was able to begin joining other women at church when she finally began using the walker in her closet! Each one launched their life of permission with a single step that set them free from bondage.

You can expect the first step into freedom to be unique to you, possibly a little uncomfortable, and definitely a move out of bondage and into freedom.

 Prayer Prompt

Father, guide me into the paths You've prepared for me, and give me wisdom and courage as I take my first step into living in the permission You offer.

WOMEN LIKE YOU

Keshia was a logistics strategy girl and had built a successful career as a corporate executive. But for years she'd been ignoring the artistic and creative gifts that God had given her. Until she didn't. Keshia had always dreamed of making candles. One weekend she gathered supplies, spread them out on her kitchen counter, and created the scent to make her first candle. That was her first step. Believing that the Lord was calling her into something new, Keshia made *one* candle. And she isn't alone! Countless times I've seen women take that first step—like the wobbly baby leaving the security of the couch, heading for Daddy's open embrace. Her first step? She made one candle.

My mom worked as a pharmacist for over thirty years. And in the last few years she was caring for her mother, my grandmama, who'd been ill. When my grandmama died a few months ago, my mother made the brave decision to step into something new. The possibility of studying counseling, and becoming a practicing counselor who helped others, had been a dream my mom had always held in her heart. But the responsibility of caring for Norman and me, and then caring for her mother, had prevented her from exploring that God-given part of her. Today my mother has taken her first step and begun her first course in counseling, opening up a whole new chapter of the life God created her to live, where she will explore and use the gifts God gave her when He created her.

I can tell you that she has *used them*—being my own go-to counselor—but now she is taking that gift to a whole new level. Her first step? A class being offered online.

When Sherrie would walk into a room of women, at a party or at a church event, she always felt insecure. And she would tell you that she desperately wanted one of those women to come speak with her and take an interest in her. I've been there; I get it. But I also know that many other women in that room felt exactly what Sherrie was feeling! So as we were chatting about it over lunch one day, I challenged Sherrie to begin to enter rooms differently. I suggested that when she walked into a space, she could ask God to show her *one woman* who needed the connection and affirmation that Sherrie had always longed for. And you know what? Sherrie received that challenge. And when she attended a reunion of sorority sisters—those she recognized and those she did not!—God showed Sherrie one woman, who was sitting alone, that she could approach. Sherrie's first step? She simply said, "Hi, I'm Sherrie. What's your name?"

When God created Brittney, He gave her a passion for whole-hearted worship. And when she worshiped at home, she sang and danced freely before the Lord. But when Brittney came to church, she became very self-conscious. When the Spirit would move her, she'd look around the room to see if others were raising their hands. To notice if anyone else was dancing. The Spirit was *moving* Brittney to dance, but because she was concerned about the opinions of others, she remained frozen. And yet as she discovered the freedom of living with permission, she responded to the Spirit's prompting by moving her body in worship before the Lord. And what began as a gentle swaying soon emerged into a reckless abandon in worship. And can I tell you what I noticed? When Brittney lived freely, others noticed and also began to live into their freedom by worshiping through dance. Brittney's first step? Ignoring the eyes of others, she released herself to give God all He deserved.

When it comes to women taking their first steps into permission living, I could go on all day! One more, one more . . .

Crystal and I had babies at the same time. In fact, the ages of her three boys match the ages of my three boys. When Crystal became pregnant with her fourth child, I knew that this was where our paths would diverge! The Greene family was complete with our three precious sons. When Crystal welcomed a daughter into her family, she had her hands full rearing those four kids. And, as you might expect, mommy world took almost everything she had. For Crystal that meant she was having a hard time learning what it looked like in this phase of life to steward her spiritual gifts in a corporate setting.

Quick detour, please: We have believed the lie that we must forsake who God has made us to be in full, or we can't be the best mom to our children. And while I applaud our commitment to rear our children well, I do not believe that honoring the other gifts God has given us in any way robs our children of the mother they need if we choose to offer the gifts at the leading of the Holy Spirit and godly counsel. In fact, the opposite is often true. When children see a mother committed to exploring the full identity God designed in her, for a purpose, they are given *permission* to do the same! A child who sees a mother or a father honoring God's unique design in their lives is one who can one day do the same—with God— for themselves. Okay, end of important detour.

I am delighted to report that Crystal took her first step by learning to ask for help with her children. And as I've watched her in that role, she has just come alive! As she honors what the Father placed in her, she is being used to touch other women's lives in powerful ways.

Because I've been so encouraged and inspired by seeing these women take their first steps into living with permission, I encourage you to begin to notice the women around you who are choosing freedom!

EXPERIMENTING

Sis, I can't say loudly enough that living with permission is a process. Before I cut my hair, I'd started experimenting with it. I took out the weave and tried a few things, tried some twists. Eventually I gathered the courage to do the big chop!

When I started using my voice, for a minute I tried to sound like Travis. If you don't know him, he's very funny. I was experimenting. But for me, trying to sound like Travis was just another version of being counterfeit. There wasn't anything wrong with that *process*, with trying to find my voice, because I knew that God was with me in it. And I ended up discovering my authentic Jackie voice.

So I encourage you to experiment. Practice something new. Try out something you've never done before. I know that trying can sometimes feel like failure, and so we're tempted to retreat. But that process is part of the journey.

When I began preaching, I'd beat myself up with self-criticism, worrying that I'd spoken too quickly or that I'd mispronounced a word. When I finished preaching, my eyes would burn with tears. After service I would go home, get in the shower, rinse away what I could, and then cry myself to sleep. When I'd pour out my heart to Travis, he'd encourage me, "Baby, you *did it* though."

The process of improvement, the process of working to get stronger, isn't fun for a perfectionist who wants to do it right the first time! But perfectionism is rooted in fear. And often it binds a person from ever starting at all.

I love encouraging women just like you to discover who they were created to be. Because the only way you will discover who you are is to try. You're going to have to get used to stumbling a little bit and then getting back up. You're going to have to look at a few tragic hairstyles. You might even start a few different businesses before you land on the right one.

Along the way, as you commit to discovering your God-given identity, you may even have to rebrand a few times! But it's worth it. Discovering who God made you to be is worth it. And as you do, you're going to discover parts you never even knew were there. This isn't a one-time interaction with God.

Continue, year after year, to ask God who He's created you to be and listen to what He reveals to you in prayer.

Prayer Prompt

Daddy, open my eyes so that I can see who You made me to be. Speak, Lord: your servant is listening.

JACKIE AT NINETEEN

It's important to notice that on any journey there are going to be hills and valleys, bumps and detours. That means that when we slide into counterfeit living, the God who remains with us is faithful to invite us back into living as the person He created us to be.

I was as powerful as a nineteen-year-old in college, when I was calling my friends together to worship, as I am today. I didn't have a degree. I didn't have a husband. But the liberated version of me you see today *lived* back then! Before I ever got stuck in performing for the approval of others, I was living as the truest version of myself. So when God called me into ministering with a microphone in my hand, the day Travis invited me to welcome folks, I was actually returning to who I was created to be from the beginning.

And that's why I want you to hear this: Harness what you have today! Notice what's inside you. What God poured into you is enough to be used today. That's not to say that it won't be perfected as you continue to walk in obedience, but what you have today is enough. In his letter to believers, Peter reminded them, "His divine power has given us everything we need for a godly life through our knowledge of him who called us by his own glory and goodness" (2 Peter 1:3).

And you can start from wherever you are. All you have to do today is take the first step.

For some, the first step will be digging a hole in the backyard garden.

For others, the first step will be purchasing the supplies they need to move forward.

For one woman, the first step will be identifying a mentor to guide her on the journey.

For another, the first step will be watching YouTube videos to learn a new skill.

And for another, the first step will be seeking forgiveness from someone they wounded.

Before we move on, I want you to ask God, "Which first step has my name on it?" Remember, God doesn't ask you to do *everything*, but He does invite you to do the *next* thing.

And did you hear a theme throughout every one of these stories? I did! Every single woman needs to get with God to discover precisely who He made her to be. Until you let the truth seep into your deep places, you'll continue to live in ways that are contrary to His design.

Begin by receiving God's love. Let yourself be identified by it. The author of Psalm 86 knew God to be "abounding in love and faithfulness" (v. 15). Abounding! As you spend time with Him, receive the great love He has for you. Then walk in the truest version of who He made you to be.

When I hosted the Exhale conference, I did it because I knew I needed to take my first step into a life of freedom. And guess what happened? The experience of taking that first step inspired me to never go back to bondage. To push through any hesitation I felt about becoming the Jackie God designed me to be. You could imagine me as that little baby, on shaky legs, waddling toward her daddy. That first step gave me a taste of freedom, and after that experience I only wanted to move forward with God in a life of permission.

And it's what I want for you too.

=== **Embrace Permission Exercise** ===

1. As you talk with God, in what direction do you think He's calling you? (For instance, the big direction might be a call to serve, or to return to school, or to mend a relationship, etc.)
2. And as you listen to God, what is the *first* step He is calling you to take? Be specific about what that first step is and when you plan to accomplish it.

=== **Prayer** ===

Let's pray together.

God, You know my heart. And You know how eager I am to race ahead on this journey! Be the One who guides my steps and lights my path. I will walk in step with You as You lead, and I will be faithful to walk in obedience. In Jesus' name, amen.

NINE

PERMISSION TO CONTINUE TO FLOURISH

The righteous will flourish like a palm tree, they will grow like a cedar of Lebanon; planted in the house of the LORD, they will flourish in the courts of our God.

PSALM 92:12–13

"BABY, DO YOU THINK WE WILL EVER START A CHURCH?"

We were living in Charlotte and Travis was away traveling. He'd called me from the airport.

I laughed. "Yes, I've always known that! I've just been waiting for God to tell you!"

Travis said that he was experiencing a holy burden. He knew that it was from God and that the call felt weighty.

So the first thing God did was confirm that we had heard Him correctly. We began to pray for direction and divine instructions. We knew He said plant a church, so we began seeking Him for the name. Travis heard the word *Forward* several times, but he kept pushing it away because he felt that it couldn't be that simple. One day, as he was sitting in front of his computer, the word *Forward* came back to his spirit. He decided to look up Forward Church to see if one already existed. At the time, there was a Forward Church in Alabama. He went and clicked on the pastors' bios. You won't believe what he saw. The pastors' names were *Travis* and *Jackie* Strickland. We knew that God was confirming His call for us to pastor Forward City Church. We had our name.

The next thing on the list was the location. Travis kept feeling God tug his heart toward Columbia, South Carolina. Columbia was a place where we knew very few people, but we knew that if God said go, we had full permission to live out everything He desired for us. We began taking trips to Columbia and started to develop a core team who shared in Bible study together and read books to prepare for the journey ahead. Travis underwent a church planter's program, and he was also in seminary at the time. God began to align people with our vision.

On the permission journey we can expect God to take us to new places. In the case of the Greene family, it was quite literally a *new place*. But the kind of newness that God invites you into might not be a geographic location!

GOD TAKES US TO NEW PLACES

Newness begets newness. That means that when God renews you from the inside out, as you recognize that new and true version of you, God takes you to new places. You start to see with new eyes. You start to recognize new opportunities.

Imagine a twenty-year marriage that's just been limping along for years. When God transforms you, He may make that marriage *new*.

As you begin to see with those new eyes, God can give you a whole new outlook on life. He might say, "You've been parked *here*, and I want to send you *here*."

Or He might whisper, "You've been taking baby steps in this direction, but now we're gonna run there together."

The Spirit might nudge you, "This way, baby. Just stick with Me."

What once looked like a limit in your life, what appeared to be a roadblock, now just looks like an entrance ramp!

Before Courtney began to live with permission, she never could have imagined welcoming a foster child into her family's home. But as God showed her who she'd been designed to be, He took her to that new place in her journey with Him.

GOD SET ME FREE AND GOD KEPT ME FREE

Now that you know my story, you know that I will testify *all day* about God calling me into ministry, into leadership. That certainly wasn't my idea—it was His! Travis and I received the call to pastor in 2013; I had to accept God's permission every step of the way! I needed God's power to offer that first welcome in worship. And the first time I preached, I was shaking and sweating profusely. I needed God with me as I took every single step. And yet as I committed to walking in freedom, God continued to show up.

When you see me speak today, I'm still the same passionate Jackie, but I'm a bit more poised. And that's because God not only set me free but He also keeps me free. With every new revelation. With every new woman's testimony of freedom that I've witnessed. God keeps pushing me, as a loving father does, not to give up on what is in me—no matter how uncomfortable the journey was or is.

The way God keeps us free is by walking with us, one step of obedience at a time.

SETTING US FREE AND KEEPING US FREE

I think you remember the glimpses I shared of my hair pain, right? For me, that experience is this before-and-after snapshot of when God gave me permission to be exactly who I was.

But as I've mentioned, the permission journey is just that: a *journey*. While it would be great if it were as simple as the before and after, our lives are a little messier than that! God knows that. And that's why He accompanies us through life.

When we stumble, God helps us to our feet.

When we believe a lie, God's Spirit speaks truth to our hearts and minds.

When we backslide, God forgives and renews.

When we veer from the path, God gently woos us back toward Himself.

For a season of my life, the word God spoke to me was "remain." And it's a word I want you to take with you. A lot of us get fired up when God shows us a new thing or invites us into something new. We start out with a bang and then we fizzle to a drizzle. We have a hot three months and then whatever ignited our new fire becomes extinguished. But that cycle, jumping from one high to the next, is not how you sustain a new way of life. The Father taught me to pray—not only for the strength to start but also the strength to stay. To remain in step with Him. To remain obedient to Him. *Because God is about sustaining, He teaches us the life of remaining!*

In John's gospel Jesus announces that He is the true vine, and His Father is the gardener. He calls out to us, "Remain in me, as I also remain in you. No branch can bear fruit by itself; it must remain in the vine. Neither can you bear fruit unless you remain in me" (John 15:4). God *remains* in us! *Because He remains with us, we remain free.*

The message of permission isn't about just launching a temporary initiative in your life. It's about beginning and continuing in a life of freedom.

Whether you relate most to Courtney, Frieda, Tammy, Pam, or Unique, there's likely one sticking point in your life where God is helping you to find freedom. And that's not a one-and-done moment. That's a process and God promises to remain with you throughout your journey. Yes, your identity as God's beloved dissolves fear. But there will be days when fear will creep up. Yes, your identity as God's beloved is the foundation for your healing, but there will be days when you'll feel the sting of those hurts He is healing.

God's good plan for your life—to use you as a vessel of the highest honor, that vision He saw when He spoke you into existence—unfolds as you remain with Him and He remains with you.

GOD GAVE ME PERMISSION
TO INVITE OTHERS

During a season of deep growth, I was fully committed to shedding all the remaining layers in my life. I wanted to do away with anything that held the potential to land me back in a place of immobility. I have always had a huge longing to become all that God desired me to be. I was very focused on this quest as we began 2017. That January, I had the pleasure of speaking at our Night of Worship at Columbia College (an all-women's college at the time). This gathering was another defining moment in ministry for me.

That night I felt as if God was daring me to go on stage and speak from my heart. Although I had prepared notes and worked through exactly what I wanted to say, I had learned how much it pays to obey God rather than stick to your own agenda. My whole message centered around letting go of the counterfeit version of yourself, the person you create in an attempt to please others. I challenged the audience to embrace the permission God gives to be the person that He created. This is the version of us that God adores. When it came time for the altar call (an invitation for prayer in response to this challenge), the entire auditorium came down front. God showed me through this that He knows just the way to touch the hearts of those He created.

I marveled that He was using me to invite others into the journey.

Not long after, I was invited to speak at the Victorious Secrets conference in Virginia. This event was one to remember. What stood out to me most was that I didn't feel afraid at all! I actually felt prepared for the moment. God is so wise in His ability to prepare us while we are completely unaware of it happening. As I traveled all around the world supporting my husband, I had no idea that these trips were training grounds for the day I would arrive to different places for my own engagements. I knew just what to expect when it came to travel, lobby calls, and so many other engagement-related things. Then when I was the speaker, rather than Travis, I continued to be amazed that God was using me to invite others into freedom!

Month after month after giving my first *yes*, the Father began to pour more and more fuel on my fire! About two months later, I was set to preach at Forward City. That morning I woke up with a strong sense of the Father's permission. It felt like a fire inside me! I decided that morning that I wanted to wear a black sleeveless dress with a white collar, black leggings, and complete the look with my black-and-white Chuck Taylors. I loved the freedom I felt the day I chose to live in the comfort of my own skin and do things the way I felt led by God to do them!

It continues to amaze me as I see what God has done with the Permission Movement. And today God is giving me more and more opportunities to share about this permission way of life! I don't know what else God has in store, but I do know that His heart is committed to continue to welcome women into freedom, in unique and lasting ways.

What I've learned along the way is that what happened to me—in those opportunities to speak a word in front of audiences—is what God invites every free woman to do: *to encourage others to live authentically and help set others free.* It may not be from a stage, but as you live in the freedom God has given you, He's welcoming you to this task. To a crowd of religious leaders who didn't welcome Him, Jesus said, "If the Son sets you free, you will be free indeed" (John 8:36). That's the *goodness* into which you're inviting others.

GOD CALLS US TO INVITE OTHERS INTO PERMISSION LIVING

I've said this before: When you are being who God uniquely designed you to be, you give other women permission to be who they really are. It's contagious! Your freedom empowers other women to see themselves in a new way. When a woman sees another woman living with permission, she starts to hunger for it herself.

That's what happened when Tammy invited Unique to brunch. Tammy had been growing in freedom, and Unique saw something in her that she wanted for herself. So when Tammy invited her to an event at Forward City, Unique was all in. Sometimes inviting others into permission is *literally* inviting them—to church, to Permission World virtually, to a Bible study, or to brunch.

Other times we're going to notice a woman who needs freedom and share with her that there's hope.

"Hey girl, you seem a little stuck. And believe me, I get it because I was there. I know what you're facing."

"I've been hurt like that."

"I've stumbled like that."

"I was in that low place too."

And then we invite her into the "something better" that we've discovered.

When the apostle Paul was writing to the believers in Corinth, he began his letter, "Praise be to the God and Father of our Lord Jesus Christ, the Father of compassion and the God of all comfort, who comforts us in all our troubles, so that we can comfort those in any trouble with the comfort we ourselves receive from God" (2 Corinthians 1:3–4). He was naming a kingdom principle: we're called to share what God gives us with others. When I see a woman who's bound by the same things with which I was bound, I'm going to grab her hand and say, "Hey, let me give you a tool that helped me find another way of life." That woman might not have known that there is a better way to live.

When Jesus came to earth, He didn't come for Himself. He came to set people free. And that's what we were created to do as well. As we walk with Him, as we bear His likeness, we set others free.

God calls us to invite others to live in freedom. Can you see the progression?

God sets you free and keeps you free.

God sends you to new places.

And God invites you to invite others into the journey. I say this all the time: free people, free people! What a privilege it is to have the opportunity to invite others into such a rich place.

As you commit to living authentically, you can expect to experience all three.

🔑 Prayer Prompt

Lord, because You have set me free and You are keeping me free, I want to invite others into this way of life. Show me who I can welcome into this abundant life.

WHAT I NEED YOU TO KNOW

Sis, I know that my story as a communicator is likely different from your story. Your freedom, your journey, your calling to invite others is definitely going to be unique to you! And it's important to me that you *feel* that freedom. Because I need you to know what matters to me more than anything else.

There's not been anything in my life more fulfilling than my relationship with God. There is nothing more valuable to me. There's nothing that touches the core of me like what I have with Him. I found safety, identity, love, and oneness with Him in a way that I haven't found anyplace else.

Not in my marriage . . .

Not as a mother . . .

Not as a dentist . . .

Not in ministry . . .

Not on social media . . .

The love and satisfaction and understanding I received from my relationship with God convinced me of my value more than anything else could.

Nothing we have is guaranteed.

Not our marriages . . .

Not our children . . .

Not our work . . .

Not our ministries . . .

Not our followers . . .

If I lose all of those, if you lose all of those, we will still have what matters most. If life steals the gifts we've been given, we still have the love of Jesus, and we will be loved with a love that does not fail.

If you have that intimacy with God, you've got the milkshake. The other stuff? That's just the cherry on top. It's the whipped cream. But if you have that intimate relationship with God, you have nourishment. Richness.

We can spend a lot of time agonizing over what we don't have, and we fail to notice and be fed by what we do have. So if you have a relationship with God, you've got everything. You have true identity, oneness, and purpose. And you can live, daily, in the power of that reality.

Prayer Prompt

God, I am pausing, in this moment, to thank and praise You for giving me all I need. You are my *everything*.

WARNING: DON'T RISK LIVING WITHOUT PERMISSION

I'm going to be very honest with you: living a life *without* permission is exhausting.

It's the woman who says yes when she should say no because she's people pleasing.

It's the woman who doesn't exercise healthy boundaries.

It's the woman who performs to impress others.

When I mentor women and see some of these signs in their lives, I'll ask them about it.

"So why did you post that? Was it to get likes or for some other reason?"

"What was your motive for saying that?"

"Do you feel that the money you make at your job makes you valuable?"

"Did you mention that to let them know you're important?"

As a woman who *is* living freely and authentically, part of my job is to help the women I love learn how to notice when they're living to please people.

And I get it. We're living in a time when social media is

a dominant factor in the lives of almost everyone. We're not going to post pictures of our ugliest bathroom moments. But we can be thoughtful about who we're serving as we post, desiring to show up on these platforms authentically. Are we using our life and social platforms to authentically encourage others? Are we sharing how God helped us through a situation?

And guess what? This is something I have to be very intentional about as well. Ensuring that my posting is always content that honors the Lord and His children. I recognize that not all people will like my social media content, but my focus is on the ones God has uniquely assigned to me.

Because living in the fullness of who God created you to be is the only way to be who you really are, I want to share a vision of what you can expect from permission living.

Expect God to take you to new places.

Expect God to both set you free and keep you free.

Expect God to call you to invite others to join the journey in living freely.

STAYING ROOTED IN PERMISSION LIVING

Living with permission isn't something to check off your to-do list. It's a daily choice that you make to live in the freedom that's yours.

And I do too!

Every single day I make decisions about how I show up as a pastor, a wife, a mother, a podcaster, a communicator, a dentist, a visionary leader of conferences, and more. And each day you're making decisions about how you show up as an employee, a friend, a daughter, a volunteer, an auntie, a neighbor, and more. In my life, every day I am seeking to discern how to live with permission in each of those spaces. It also means that the enemy is whispering in my ear, *You're not enough.*

You're not enough relationally.

You're not enough physically.

You're not enough spiritually.

You're not enough professionally.

Are you hearing this? The enemy's strategy is to keep us from living with permission by wiggling into our hearts and minds to convince us that we're not enough.

But permission says I'm enough. You're enough. And in permission there is abundance!

Permission means that I allow myself to rest.

Permission means that I accept that what I'm able to offer to others is enough.

Permission means that when I'm faithfully attending to one thing I don't beat myself up for not doing all the things.

Permission even means that I practice self-care.

And when I do, when I receive the permission God has given me, I'm finally able to be the best version of myself: for God, for others, and for me.

Sis, I have to be daily nourished by God's truth just like

you! Every day I have to practice living freely and authentically. And what that looks like is implementing all the practices of living with freedom: the four pillars, the three daily choices, the practical steps that propel us forward in the journey. Living with permission is about making these choices day in and day out.

But I do want you to know that the fight is real. It's real and it's happening in the spiritual realm. Paul reminded us that "our struggle is not against flesh and blood, but against the rulers, against the authorities, against the powers of this dark world and against the spiritual forces of evil in the heavenly realms" (Ephesians 6:12). If you're living with permission, you can expect that the enemy is going to come for you. And you know what? You can handle it. The Spirit equips you to discern the serpent's lying voice and to choose what's most true: the reality that you are God's beloved. So if the enemy is loud in your ear, it's likely because you're right where you should be.

When the voice of the enemy is shouting at me, accusing me, I'll pause and pull away from all the noise. I'll slow down to listen for God's voice. My spiritual father, Pastor Matthew, has taught me to apply the words of Jesus in those moments: "Every plant that my heavenly Father has not planted will be pulled up by the roots" (Matthew 15:13). That means that if there is anything growing in my life that was not planted by the Father, it needs to be pulled up by the roots. Even if it's a small little weed just beginning to sprout. So I have become much better at identifying these foreign weeds that are trying to claim residence in the garden of my heart and mind. And I don't just cut them back. No, I go to the Lord and ask Him to pull the lie up by the root!

And I want to encourage you to create that space in your life as well, where you can offer those words of the enemy to our Father. Maybe you'll step into the shower to find the silence to listen to God. Or you might ask Alexa to play a worship song that God has put on your heart. If you're at work you might take a break, slip in your AirPods, and engage in worship. Or you might notice that God is leading you to pick up the phone and call someone. There are so many ways that God will affirm you in those hard moments, when you take the time to stop and be with Him.

When I go to that quiet space, the Lord always reminds me that—as I learned from Bobby Schuller—I'm not what I do; I'm not what I have; I'm not what people say about me. And then I soak in God's love, receiving it in my deep places. I'll spend time in prayer. I may fast. Basically, I slow down to listen for God's voice. And when I'm refilled, I'll jump back in.

CABO

A few years ago, my husband and I celebrated the thirty-eighth birthday of his best friend by joining two other couples in Cabo San Lucas, Mexico. The day before we were to head home, we decided to go on an ATV ride. Based on the advertisement, we thought it would be a relaxing excursion. But we quickly found out this couldn't be further from the truth! After setting off, led by a few local guides, we started to encounter steep hills. We were climbing the side of a mountain with narrow paths.

Not long after we'd begun, one of the girls in our group had trouble with her bike. Because the vehicles stirred up so much dust, it was difficult to see the person in front of you or behind. When I couldn't see my friend, I stopped and got off my bike to see if I could spot her.

"No, amiga!" the guide warned. "*Es muy peligroso!*" (If I hadn't understood his Spanish, I could see from the fear on his face what he was communicating: it is very dangerous!) He explained that because there were wild animals, we needed to remain on the bikes. After having trouble with her bike, my friend decided to get in the safety car that traveled along with the group. And then there were five of us.

As we climbed higher and higher, the terrain beside the path dropped off as a steep cliff.

When the guides gave us a break at the peak of this mountainous desert, we were allowed to stop and take pictures. During our photo shoot, they showed us a white bush called a *palo blanco* tree. Its bark contains a protective serum that's like sunscreen, to protect skin from the sun. Following the guides' lead, we spread it over our hands, arms, and faces.

After our break, we turned around to descend the mountain. We were only about one hundred yards from the finish line: the beach where we would be totally done with the rough, winding path through the mountain, where we could relax and eat.

Travis was in front of me, but when he could no longer spot me, he yelled, "Baby! Are you okay?" Between the sound of the vehicles and the clouds of dust, it was difficult to communicate.

When I heard his voice, I answered, "I don't feel well. I feel weak."

The last words I remember him saying were, "Okay, baby, try to keep up . . ."

Less than thirty seconds later, I blacked out.

When I came to, my bike was flying through the air, headed toward the cliff of a mountain. Alert enough to sense pending death, I quickly assessed that if I continued to hold on to the handlebars of the bike, I'd die.

So I jumped.

Mind you, I wasn't jumping onto a pile of leaves or into the ocean. The mountainous terrain was like a stark desert. No vegetation. Nothing.

And yet instead of landing on the hard ground, I was propelled into the one bush in the area, a palo blanco.

I was groggy, but I could hear Travis calling my name. By the time he reached me, he was bloodied by briars.

"Is she conscious? Is she conscious?" I heard him begin to scream after seeing me.

And because of my medical training, I weirdly answered to give them the best information: "I'm hurting really bad, but it all feels superficial."

The fact was, there was blood everywhere. I was cut, bruised, broken. The impact of being thrown into the bush was brutal. I was so far down the hill an ambulance could never have reached me. So Travis and another guy helped me to my feet and walked me up the hill to the waiting safety car.

I'd been in shock, but the moment the car started driving I broke down, crying uncontrollably and hyperventilating.

When we reached a hospital, I was diagnosed with only a sprained neck. The guides had stayed with us, and they reported that they'd seen accidents much less severe in which people had been paralyzed or killed. Baffled, they didn't understand how I'd survived. Knowing the area, they said that had I crashed into any other tree or bush it would have shattered my bones, but the palo blanco is flexible.

That night, exhausted, I was amazed at who God had been for me in that moment. He was Jehovah Sabaoth. Jehovah is God's name, and "Sabaoth" is a military charge that signals God is waging war. What it meant to me was that He does not play when it comes to those who belong to Him. He is King of kings and Lord of lords. The God of angel armies who wages war on my behalf. In the most unlikely circumstance, God had protected me, preserving the call on my life.

Flipping my car as a teenager hadn't taken me out, and God had preserved my life once again. Both rescues confirmed my purpose. God needed *Jackie*—the woman He designed so carefully and intricately—to bring to the world what only I can bring.

And the same is true of you. There is something in you,

created when you were in your mama's womb, that no one else can offer to the world. We need what only you can bring. Maybe you haven't had life-threatening accidents in motor vehicles, but perhaps there's been something else that threatened to take you out. Maybe it was a divorce that made you want to give up on life. Maybe you felt as though the loss of a loved one would do you in. Or perhaps your own life was physically at risk. But if you are reading these words, your life was preserved because what you are bringing to the world is absolutely necessary. God is inviting you to live fully and authentically so that the call on your life—the one no one else can execute—*will* be fulfilled.

The result of my near-death experience in Cabo: In response to God's goodness in my life, I dug my heels even further into this life of permission to which I'd been called and have been called to invite other women. That evening I committed to shout and scream and wave the permission banner higher than ever before to let people know that the God I serve is a freeing God, and also a sustaining God who will continue what He began, causing it to come to completion because it's His work.

I believe that God saved my life so that I could share this message with you. The fact that I was so close to death, and yet God preserved me, makes me live each day with greater focus and intentionality. To ensure when it's my time to go be with the Lord, every woman I was assigned to give the invitation to the life of permission will have it.

Sister, if God has work on this earth for you to do, if you've not yet fulfilled your unique assignment—the one that only you can do, because you were so carefully designed by God—it ain't over for you yet.

YOU ARE BELOVED

You ready to live this life? Ready or not, here it comes!

Sister, your permission journey with the Lord isn't going to look like mine. It's not going to look like your best friend's journey with Him. Living in the freedom God has given you is going to look unique because *you are unique!* When God formed you, He did it intimately, intricately, and precisely. God made no mistake in the careful way He crafted you. You are exactly what He wanted you to be. No matter what lies the enemy whispers about who you are, what is most true is that you are a gift that the Master treasures, because you are exactly as He intended. You are exactly the daughter He wanted. You are His beloved.

So I want to share a final thought from Bobby Schuller:

You are loved by God. You always have been, and you always will be. He was there when you were born, and he'll be there to catch your last breath. Your accomplishments don't matter to him as much as your smile. Your treasures only matter to him because they matter to you. You're his treasure. He also doesn't care about your reputation. He simply longs to be with you. He calls you beloved.[3]

Do you believe it? Do you know that it's true in your deepest places?

It is.

You are the beloved of God.

I pray that in these pages you have been persuaded to grab hold of who you really are. You must fight to eradicate the need to have others say what the Father has already declared about you. God has been singing the same song over you for your entire life. In fact, "The LORD your God is with you, the Mighty Warrior who saves. He will take great delight in you; in his love he will no longer rebuke you, but will rejoice over you with singing" (Zephaniah 3:17). Some seasons we are just more in tune to hear it. I pray that you will rediscover the God-created version of yourself that is untainted by the pressures and opinions of the outside world. I pray that you will live to delight in the smile of your Father in heaven! After closing this book, you'll have the opportunity to open a new chapter of your story. The one that is true. The one that is real. The one that is authentic.

My dear friend, you have full permission. I dare you to live free!

WITH LOVE,
DR. JACKIE

═ **Embrace Permission Exercise** ═

Spend time in God's presence. Receive His love. Experience His affirmation. Notice His smile of delight. Enjoy His care.
Repeat tomorrow.
And the next day.
And the next.

═ **Prayer** ═

Let's pray together.

Daddy, I am committed to being fully and precisely who You made me to be. You have given me everything I need. Planted and rooted in You, I will flourish like a palm tree and be strong like a cedar of Lebanon. Thank You for calling me Your beloved daughter. In Jesus' name, amen.

STATEMENT OF PERMISSION

WHEN YOU WANT TO AFFIRM WHAT IS MOST TRUE ABOUT *who God has made you to be, use this Statement of Permission to speak aloud, or transcribe in your journal, your identity as one uniquely created by God to live free. (Sign your name at the bottom as an act of agreement!)*

I was carefully designed by God to be exactly who He intended me to be. Because He is my Maker, I am worthy. He loves me simply because I am His.

While I was made for freedom, I fell into the bondage of sin and death. I've been wounded. I've cared too much about the opinions of others. And I've sinned. In these ways, I've failed to embrace the freedom that is my birthright. As a result, I've lived a counterfeit life, settling for less than God's best. I've behaved as if I'm less than, more than, or other than who He has made me to be. I accepted fear, comfort, trauma, people-pleasing, and unsupported living as normal.

But God has never stopped calling me into the life of freedom He meant for me to have from the beginning of the world. Moment by moment He is always inviting me to be the person He created me to be. God's Holy Spirit opens the eyes and ears of my heart to the ways in which I am bound. And because of those promptings, I will live a life of sustained freedom! I won't just start free; I will stay free! I will remain!

I belong to God, and I am His beloved. This is the truest thing about me and nothing can change this reality. Because I am fully received by God, I have permission from Him to be who He designed me to be.

I've come to understand that God can't heal what I hide, so I choose to live in truth daily.

I know that to remain in freedom, anything not planted by the Father must be pulled up by the roots, and I'm committed to allowing the Father to do this work daily in my heart.

I'm committed to letting God clothe me in the dressing room of prayer, to removing all unnecessary layers there.

The pillars that support me as I live freely are prayer, scripture, obedience, and faith. Grounded in these practices, I choose to live every day with authenticity, transparency, and in the bond of community. Moment by moment, I know that God loves me and He's with me!

As a woman who lives according to the permission that God has given, I have been set free and God sustains me day by day. He is taking me to new places and allowing me to experience life on new levels. And He is encouraging me to invite others into the permission journey and the reality of

His love for them. Free people, free people! I will forever wave high the banner of permission!

Now and forever, I am precisely and fully who God created me to be.

_____

(Name, Date)

ACKNOWLEDGMENTS

NELSON BOOKS, YOU HAVE AN EXCEPTIONAL TEAM. I WANT to extend the hugest thank-you to every person in your organization who had a hand in making this book what it is. A special thanks to my editor, Janet Talbert. It means everything that you believed so much in the permission message, that you fought for it to be heard. You were the greatest coach, prayer warrior, and encourager in this journey of publishing my first nationally released literary work.

Lisa and Denise, thank you both for having a huge hand in making what was once just a good idea into a reality. You made it clear that the messages on my heart and the heart of my husband needed to be heard, and you went out to ensure that we landed the right partnership. You have given the best legal and literary representation ever.

Lastly to the MVP of MVPs, Margot Starbucks. You put your whole heart into making *Permission to Live Free* what it is. Thank you for having the patience to thoroughly hear my heart and learn my voice so you could help me pen and restructure my life's message. You helped to ensure that every woman who would need to find herself in these pages felt fully represented. I will forever hold dear every call, text, email, voice memo, and Zoom call!

To my incredible parents: Cynthia and Willie Ware, and Dr. Yaw Gyamfi. Thank you for giving and helping to shape my life, but more importantly for birthing a hunger in me to know God in a way that is real, authentic, and transformative. Every sacrifice, godly deposit, and encouraging word has helped to propel my spiritual walk. Mama, I personal thank you for being my greatest example of living authentically in relationship with the Lord. I am in so many ways because you are!

To my spiritual parents, pastors Matthew and Mona Thompson, God could not have been more gracious to my husband and me than when He decided to bless our lives with your leadership and love. You have both challenged me to live with permission in every single area of my life.

To my mother-in-love, you are one of my greatest cheerleaders and I will never take your heart for me for granted. To all my siblings, thank you for all the ways you have supported and encouraged me. Your presence in my life means everything! To my spiritual daughters, thank you for never allowing me to give up. So many times it was your faces, your texts, and your help with my babies that kept me going. Dajia, you deserve double honor for the way you have helped me give my boys the best, while also ensuring that I had space to obey the instruction of the Lord in the many other areas of my life.

To the greatest team on the planet, the DrJG / Forward City squad. Because of you so many amazing things have been produced, which the world has experienced through my husband and me. It's been your hands, minds, hearts, prayers, tears, and endless support and sacrifice. I know that we have the greatest team on the planet, and I do my best to let you all know how special each of you are to me. A very special shoutout to Jahniyah, Keshia, D'Nar, Matt, and Tay. From the front cover to the back, your thumbprints are all over this work. Thank you! No one has pushed the vision of DrJG Forward quite like you. Jahniyah, thank you for the million ways you helped to make this book and every other thing in my heart come to life.

To every partner of Forward City Church and every woman of the permission banner, thank you for your endless support and belief in me. I wake up daily to do my best to serve you well in all that I do.

To the Greene Team, my hearts and greatest treasures! I love you with all of me. Thank you for every sacrifice and word of encouragement.

Lastly, to my beloved Granny Katie. Your life and legacy live on through the words penned in this book. You taught me so much, yet you said so little. You always let your life speak for you. Thank you for all that it taught me!

NOTES

1. Bobby Schuller, *You Are Beloved: Living in the Freedom of God's Grace, Mercy, and Love* (Nashville: Thomas Nelson, 2018), x.
2. James Orr, ed., *International Standard Bible Encyclopedia* (Chicago: Howard-Severance Co., 1915), s.v. "Obedience, obey," available on "Obedience; Obey," Bible Study Tools, accessed October 12, 2022, https://www.biblestudytools.com /dictionary/obedience-obey/.
3. Bobby Schuller, *You Are Beloved: Living in the Freedom of God's Grace, Mercy, and Love* (Nashville: Thomas Nelson, 2018), 3.

ABOUT THE AUTHOR

AS A WIFE, MOTHER, PASTOR, *AND* DENTIST, DR. JACQUELINE "Jackie" Greene is an inspirational speaker and faith leader focused on emboldening women to own their God-given individuality. Through her permission movement, Dr. Jackie empowers women to be brave enough to step into the lives God has prepared for them. Along with her husband, Grammy-nominated recording artist Travis Greene, Jackie co-pastors the fast-growing Forward City Church in Columbia, South Carolina. Jackie and Travis are the proud parents of three sons: David Jace, Travis Joshua, and Jonathan Judah Willie.